HTML 3.2
Visual Quick Reference
Third Edition

Dean Scharf

HTML 3.2 Visual Quick Reference, Third Edition

Library of Congress Catalog No.: 97-65029

ISBN: 0-7897-1103-6

99 98 97   6 5 4 3 2

Interpretation of the printing code: the rightmost double-digit number is the year of the book's printing; the rightmost single-digit number, the number of the book's printing. For example, a printing code of 97-1 shows that the first printing of the book occurred in 1997.

Screen reproductions in this book were created using Capture from Mainstay, Camarillo, CA, and Collage Plus from Inner Media, Inc., Hollis, NH.

President Roland Elgey

Publisher Stacy Hiquet

Editorial Services Director Elizabeth Keaffaber

Managing Editor Sandy Doell

Director of Marketing Lynn E. Zingraf

Acquisitions Manager Cheryl D. Willoughby

Publishing Manager
Jim Minatel

Acquisitions Editor
Jane Brownlow

Senior Product Development Specialist
Steven M. Schafer

Production Editor
William McManus

Assistant Product Marketing Managers
Karen Hagen
Christy M. Miller

Technical Editor
Jim O'Donnell

Technical Specialist
Nadeem Muhammed

Software Relations Coordinator
Susan D. Gallagher

Editorial Assistant
Andrea Duvall

Book Designer
Kim Scott

Cover Designer
Nathan Clement

Production Team
Nicole Ruessler
Sossity Smith
Staci Somers
Paul Wilson

Indexer
Nick Schroeder

Composed in *Stone Serif* and *Helvetica* by Que Corporation.

About the Author

Dean Scharf is a creative director. He directs and supervises all phases of a project from concept to implementation. Recent projects have included books (*The Wall Street Journal* guides), interactive information kiosks, multimedia CD-ROM, and online interfaces.

Dean Scharf has worked in the fields of interactive media, advertising, corporate identity, and simplified communications. He has more than 20 years experience in design, production, planning, scheduling, execution, and delivery of print, artwork, and photography. Mr. Scharf has converted traditional design studios into state-of-the-art desktop-publishing facilities.

Dean has worked in a variety of design firms and corporate design departments, including Siegel & Gale, CBS Records, Clairol, Chermayeff and Geismar, and Donovan and Green.

Mr. Scharf studied art history and architecture at Columbia University in New York City. He continues to paint and exhibit his art work.

Acknowledgments

I would like to thank

Beverly for liking the idea originally,

Jane for making it easy,

Steven for making sure I know what I'm writing about,

Bill for making me look like I know how to spell and punctuate,

Design and Production for getting this book to press,

Krista for listening to me rant and rave a third time,

Aroma for her patience, and

Timber for distracting me.

We'd Like to Hear from You!

As part of our continuing effort to produce books of the highest possible quality, Que would like to hear your comments. To stay competitive, we *really* want you, as a computer book reader and user, to let us know what you like or dislike most about this book or other Que products.

You can mail comments, ideas, or suggestions for improving future editions to the address below, or send us a fax at (317) 581-4663. For the online inclined, Macmillan Computer Publishing has a forum on CompuServe (type **GO QUEBOOKS** at any prompt) through which our staff and authors are available for questions and comments. The address of our Internet site is **http://www.quecorp.com** (World Wide Web).

In addition to exploring our forum, please feel free to contact me personally to discuss your opinions of this book: I'm **sschafer@que.mcp.com** on the Internet.

Thanks in advance—your comments will help us to continue publishing the best books available on computer topics in today's market.

Steven M. Schafer
Senior Product Development Specialist
Que Corporation
201 W. 103rd Street
Indianapolis, Indiana 46290
USA

Contents

Part III Forms

Part VII Posting Pages

Part VIII Getting Your Files Noticed

Part IX Appendixes

Preface

Once upon a time not too long ago, I was trying to find information about something new called HTML. I knew it was a programming language for publishing documents on the World Wide Web, a graphical part of the Internet. And I knew I had to learn Web programming to keep up with the changes in the publishing industry.

I asked around and found a few facts. First, I found out that there wasn't a good book available. Perhaps you've had the same experience. Surfing the Web for documentation. Scouring bookstore shelves for a simple HTML book.

Eventually I found what I needed on the Web and on bookstore shelves. However, what I found was not clear or concise. I could see that HTML programming was easy to understand but that the documentation wasn't. I just wanted to know what code to type and how to use it. What are the limitations? How do I specify type, control graphic design, insert images, and link files? And I wanted it in a book that was easy to use.

So I found the simple answers and put them in the first edition of this book. In this edition I have included new tags that are now a part of the HTML language.

Each set of facing pages presents one topic. I include some information on posting pages, where to find servers, how to structure documents, and a few design tips, but the bulk of the book focuses on the code. You can go pretty far on the basics because there isn't much more to HTML programming than the basics.

This book is for anyone who wants to get started with HTML and for people who want a quick reference at their side. You don't need a week to learn HTML basics. Just an hour, this book, a word processor, and a browser will do.

Buy this book if you want to

- Understand how Web pages are created
- Find the simple facts about Web programming
- Create Web pages of your own
- Have a quick reference to check as you program
- Learn more programming techniques
- Make the transition from desktop publishing to online publishing
- Establish a presence on the Internet for your business

- Get informed before hiring an Internet programmer
- Spend less than what other books cost

If you want a deeper understanding of HTML programming and the World Wide Web after you read this book, Que has published several related books that should be of interest:

Special Edition Using HTML 3.2, Third Edition

Special Edition Using Netscape 3

Special Edition Using the Internet, Third Edition

Special Edition Using MS Internet Explorer 3

Running a Perfect Web Site, Second Edition

Platinum Edition, Using HTML 3.2, Java 1.1, and CGI

All these books should be available at your local bookstore. You can also find information about these and other Que books on the Web at **http://www.quecorp.com**, the Macmillan Information SuperLibrary.

Dean Scharf

What Is HTML?

HTML is a mark-up, or formatting, language. In fact, *HTML* stands for *Hypertext Markup Language*. You mark up text files with HTML tags so that they can be read over a network or locally on your computer by browsing software. Tags are pieces of code surrounded by the symbols < and >. Browsers read tags when formatting HTML files on your screen. Documents available on the World Wide Web are HTML files.

HTML does not describe a page the way some computer languages do. Some languages actually describe every graphic element and its position on the page. This includes fonts, point sizes, screen values, line weights, and so on. In contrast, HTML describes neither text or graphic elements nor their exact placement. HTML only *tags* the content of the file with certain attributes that are later defined by the browser used to view the file. It is like a person who writes a memo by hand and puts small comments before certain sections of the memo to indicate to the secretary specific things to do—for example, "new paragraph here," "new page," "please highlight this sentence," and so on.

HTML tags attribute type styles, insert graphics, sound, and video files in the text, and create hypertext links and forms. *Hypertext* is the most important capability of the HTML language. It means that any piece of text or graphic can link to another HTML document.

The official HTML language is a specific set of tags that all browsers should interpret. Some browsers are capable of interpreting additional tags outside the standard. New tags are added to the standard set over time.

Mosaic, one of the first browsers, was developed by the National Center for Supercomputing Applications (NSCA) at the University of Illinois. It combined color graphics with HTML text capabilities for the first time. These days Netscape Navigator, developed by people formerly at NSCA, has become the browser of choice because of its speed and enhanced features. Microsoft's Internet Explorer is gaining ground fast. Some access providers have developed their own browsers.

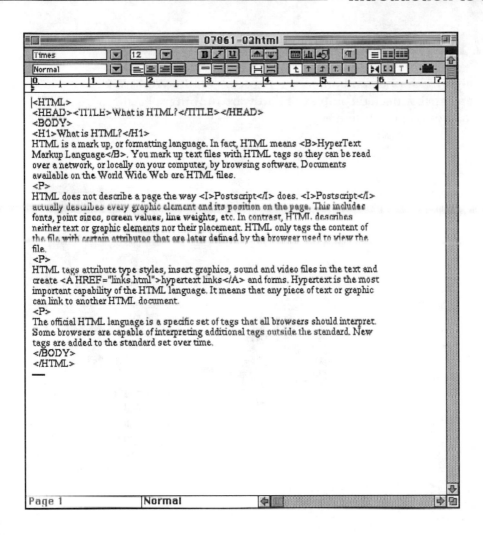

```
<HTML>
<HEAD><TITLE>What is HTML?</TITLE></HEAD>
<BODY>
<H1>What is HTML?</H1>
HTML is a mark up, or formatting language. In fact, HTML means <B>HyperText
Markup Language</B>. You mark up text files with HTML tags so they can be read
over a network, or locally on your computer, by browsing software. Documents
available on the World Wide Web are HTML files.
<P>
HTML does not describe a page the way <I>Postscript</I> does. <I>Postscript</I>
actually describes every graphic element and its position on the page. This includes
fonts, point sizes, screen values, line weights, etc. In contrast, HTML describes
neither text or graphic elements nor their placement. HTML only tags the content of
the file with certain attributes that are later defined by the browser used to view the
file.
<P>
HTML tags attribute type styles, insert graphics, sound and video files in the text and
create <A HREF="links.html">hypertext links</A> and forms. Hypertext is the most
important capability of the HTML language. It means that any piece of text or graphic
can link to another HTML document.
<P>
The official HTML language is a specific set of tags that all browsers should interpret.
Some browsers are capable of interpreting additional tags outside the standard. New
tags are added to the standard set over time.
</BODY>
</HTML>
```

How HTML Works on the Web

Like e-mail, FTP, Gopher, and other Internet services, the World Wide Web requires an interconnected complex of hardware running specialized software to work on the Internet.

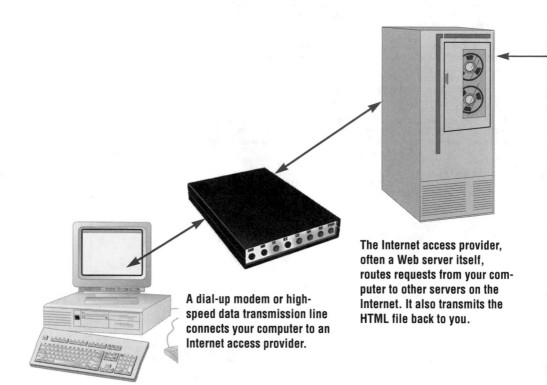

A dial-up modem or high-speed data transmission line connects your computer to an Internet access provider.

The Internet access provider, often a Web server itself, routes requests from your computer to other servers on the Internet. It also transmits the HTML file back to you.

The browser on your computer sends requests for HTML files to remote servers on the Internet by using addresses called *URLs* (Uniform Resource Locators). When the data returns to your computer, the browser interprets the HTML tags and displays the formatted text along with any graphics.

The Internet is a worldwide network of servers. Your request bounces from server to server until the URL address of the HTML file you want is found. The data then returns over the Internet to your computer.

The Web server holds the IITML filc you are looking for along with any other files needed by the file, including graphic, sound, and video files inserted in it and associated programs known as gateway scripts. *Gateway scripts* are programs running on the server that process data.

How Browsers Work

Browsers send requests and receive the data needed to display the HTML page on your screen. This includes the HTML file itself plus all the graphic, sound, and video files mentioned in it. Once the data is retrieved, the browser formats the type as indicated by the HTML tags and displays it with the graphics files on your computer screen.

When you click a hypertext link, a new request to retrieve another file is sent out over the Internet. Most browsers perform other functions, such as sending e-mail or downloading files via FTP. *Helper applications* on your computer, plug-ins, and enhancements like Java enable the browser to play sound and video inserted in the HTML file.

The fonts installed on your computer and the display preferences in the browser you use determine how text is formatted.

HTML files look like a mix of text and coding when viewed in a word processing program. The code is comprised of symbols and acronyms interspersed with text and file titles.

Graphics, sound, or video files are not actually part of the HTML document, however, their titles are used. The file title and location (also called a *path*) tell the browser what to retrieve and where to find it (see page 86).

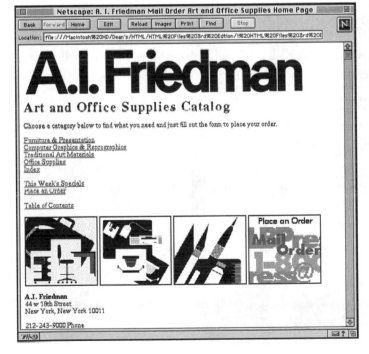

The browser combines the formatted text with inline graphics and highlights the linked elements. It displays them on your screen as a graphical point-and-click interface.

Different Browsers

All browsers perform the same basic functions: they send requests to remote Web servers, receive the data, and display formatted HTML files on your computer screen. But that's where the similarity ends. Some don't do anything else. In fact, they don't even display proportional fonts or graphics. These are called *non-graphical browsers*. Others have features beyond the basics. They display graphics and forms, send e-mail, download files via FTP, and play sound and video. These are called *graphical browsers*.

You must use a browser written for your operating system. Browsers are available for all major systems. You can download a browser at one of the FTP sites listed in the following table. (Some of these browsers are free; others need to be paid for if you continue to use them.)

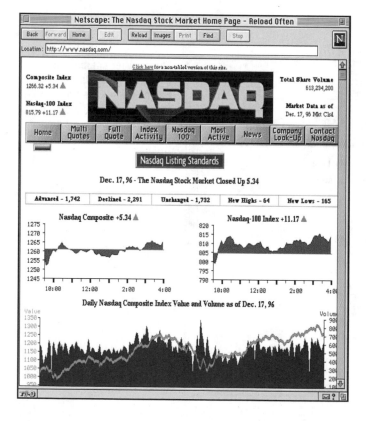

Graphical browsers format text with proportional fonts. They insert inline graphics and highlight hypertext links in color. The browser displays all the text and graphic elements on your screen in a point-and-click interface.

FTP Sites for Web Browsers

Browser	Platforms Supported	URL or FTP Address	Directory
Netscape	Windows, Macintosh, UNIX	**ftp.netscape.com** **http://home.net-scape.com**	/pub
Mosaic	Windows, Macintosh, UNIX	**ftp.ncsa.uiuc.edu**	/Web/Mosaic
DOS Lynx	DOS	**ftp2.cc.ukans.edu**	/pub/WWW/DosLynx
Lynx	UNIX	**sunsite.unc.edu**	/pub/packages/ infosystems/WWW/ clients/lynx
Microsoft Internet Explorer	Windows, Macintosh	**http://www. microsoft.com/ie/**	

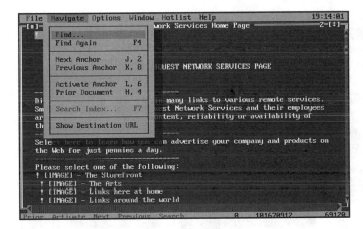

Non-graphical browsers usually display text with mono-spaced fonts. They substitute alternate text for inline graphics.

What's Out There?

A great variety of information, products, and services are available on the Web. Sources range from government to industry, from commerce to colleges, and from publishers to research institutes.

If the source is the United States government, the information—whether text, sound, video, or imagery—is public domain. You can use it any way you want (because our tax dollars paid for it in the first place). This doesn't apply to everything across the board, however, because some information may have been privately funded but made available through government sources by special arrangement. Files should have information to clarify possible uses. Check with the agency making the material available if you are unsure of its public domain status.

Lots of free software and support is available on the Web. Some of it is product specific and supplied by individual hardware manufacturers.

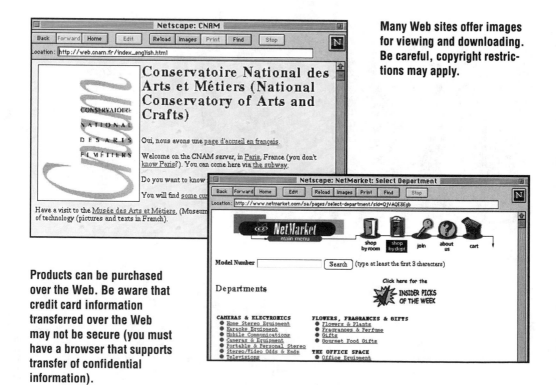

Many Web sites offer images for viewing and downloading. Be careful, copyright restrictions may apply.

Products can be purchased over the Web. Be aware that credit card information transferred over the Web may not be secure (you must have a browser that supports transfer of confidential information).

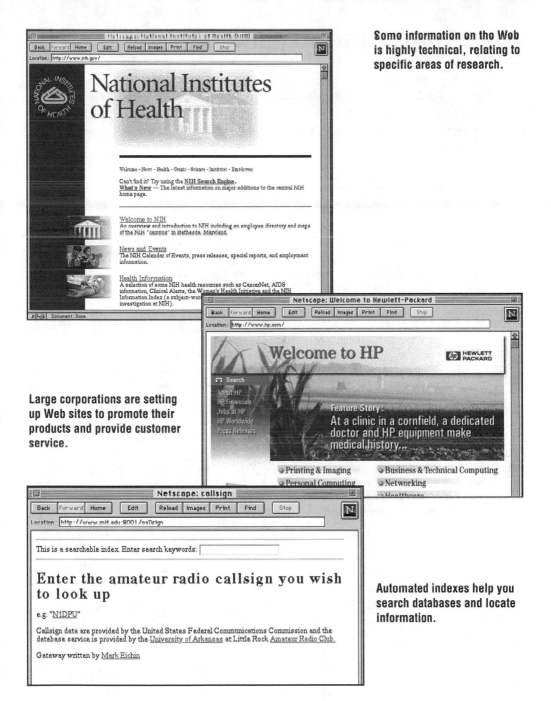

Some information on the Web is highly technical, relating to specific areas of research.

Large corporations are setting up Web sites to promote their products and provide customer service.

Automated indexes help you search databases and locate information.

What You Need To Learn

There are four criteria you need to fulfill to become an HTML electronic publisher: you need to get the right hardware and software; learn the HTML programming language; understand how to structure Web documents; and find a server to post your pages on. Don't panic. None of these are rocket science.

If you have a computer and you are on the Net already, you probably have this area covered. If you intend to include graphics, sound, and video in your documents, you will need software to create or manipulate these files (see page 16).

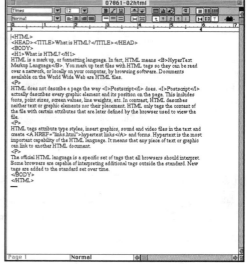

If you know how to type, you can program using HTML. The catch is you just have to know *what* to type (see pages 20-145).

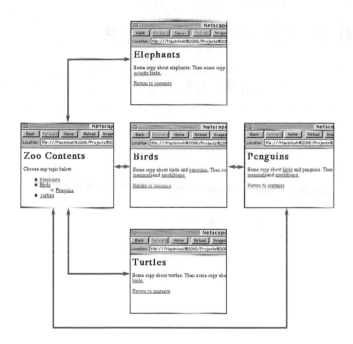

There are only two choices when structuring documents: linear, like a book, and non-linear, like a road map (see pages 146-151). Use linear structures to control the order in which information is viewed, for example, a lesson. Use non-linear structures (as shown here) to allow a person to determine the order in which they view the information from the possibilities you provide, for example, a table of contents.

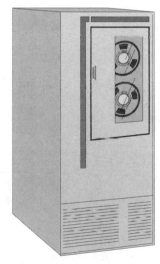

When you find a server to post your pages on, you can download your files and customize any gateway scripts needed. A system administrator can do the parts you don't know how to complete (see pages 166-167).

What You Need To Write or Browse

Writing for the Web and browsing it require some of the same hardware and software, depending on what you want to do. You can write documents that use text and no graphics, sound, or video. You can also browse without the graphics, sound, and video. It's up to you.

To write HTML files, you really only need a word processor, as HTML files are just text files. However, you may want to get HTML authoring software that is

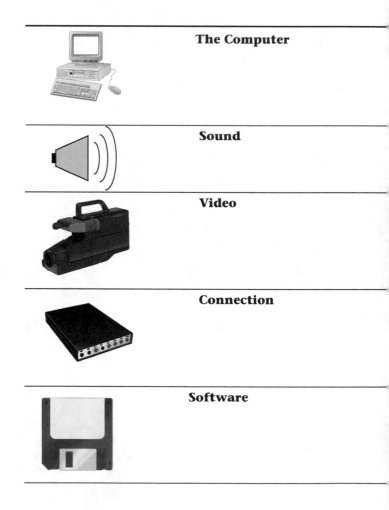

The Computer

Sound

Video

Connection

Software

designed to automate some of the typing. To create or edit graphics, sound, and video, you need to have the appropriate hardware and software for working with these files.

To browse, you need a browser program for your operating system, a connection to an access provider, and whatever additional hardware and software that may be needed to view the graphics, sound, and video files you encounter.

Writing	Browsing
Almost any computer that runs a word processor will do.	Processor speed and RAM are the most important factors no matter what platform you choose. Buy or upgrade as much as you can afford.
Sound board and audio software only if you intend to create and edit files.	Sound board and audio software only if you intend to listen to sound when included in files.
Video board and software only if you intend to create and edit files.	Video board will improve speed but may not be needed to view video.
No connection is needed to write or post files to a server; you can send them to the server on disk. Often a large project with many graphics is impractical to move any other way.	You must have a connection to an Internet access provider (the faster the better).
Any word processing software that saves text files will do for HTML programming, or use HTML authoring software. To check your files locally you need a browser.	Any graphic or non-graphical browser for your platform. Sound and video players if you intend to view these.

Connections

You connect to the Internet via a data transmission line. Lines vary in speed and cost: the faster the line the more expensive the cost. Pick one that fits your budget and needs. The chart on this page lists options in increasing speed and expense. Localtalk and Ethernet are included in the chart for comparison because they do not connect to the Internet directly but are used in local area networks. Transmission speed is limited by the slowest link between your computer and the Internet. You need to match the speed of your computer with the speed of connection and balance that against needed throughput.

Check with the network administrator where you work or study before you spend any money. The equipment and connections you need may already be available to you. Most large corporations, government agencies, research institutes, and colleges

Type	Speed	User
Modem 14.4 Kbps, dial-up connection to access provider	14.4 Kbps, about 1.5 pages of text	individual at home or in the office, used for all Internet services
Modem 28.8 Kbps, dial-up connection to access provider	28.8 Kbps, about 3 pages of text	individual at home or in the office, used for all Internet services
Switch 56, dedicated line, connected to point of presence	56 Kbps, about 6 pages of text	corporations
ISDN, dedicated line, connected to point of presence	64 Kbps, about 8 pages of text	corporations home use in some areas
Localtalk, local area network, must connect to point of presence	230 Kbps, about 25 pages of text	corporations, businesses, schools
T1, dedicated line, connected to point of presence	1.54 Mbps, a short book	corporations, research institutes, universities
Ethernet, local area network, must connect to point of presence	10 Mbps, a long book	corporations, research institutes, universities
T3, dedicated line, connected to point of presence	45 Mbps, the complete works of Shakespeare	corporations, research institutes, universities
FDDI, dedicated line, connected to point of presence	100 Mbps, the Oxford English Dictionary	corporations, research institutes, universities

and universities have high-speed lines connecting their network to the Internet
Ask the network administrator for information about how to use them.

A simple modem plugged into your telephone jack is the least expensive connection method, but it is also the slowest. It is easy to purchase and install. You can set up the equipment yourself and have the monthly Internet access fees charged to a credit card. If you can only afford a dial-up connection to an Internet access provider, get a fast modem. Spending a little more for the fastest modem will save you money in the long run. A faster modem means quicker data transfers, shorter connect times, and lower bills.

High-end dedicated lines are expensive but fast. Speed allows not only faster transmission time but also more people to work at the same time. Large corporations and universities can afford a dedicated line like a T1 connection. These involve special equipment and software between your network and the Internet's closest point of presence.

Provider	Cost
purchased by user	local call rates of your telephone company
purchased by user	local call rates of your telephone company
local telecommunications company	dependent on distance, charged per mile per month
local telecommunications company	dependent on distance, charged per mile per month
corporations, businesses, schools	cost of installation
corporations, research institutes, universities, government	dependent on distance, charged per mile per month
corporations, research institutes, universities, government	cost of installation
corporations, research institutes, universities, government	dependent on distance, charged per mile per month
corporations, research institutes, universities, government	dependent on distance, charged per mile per month

Basic HTML Programming Elements

HTML documents consist of two basic parts: the head and the body. Both the head and the body use pieces of code called tags. *Tags* style text, link files, embed graphics, insert tables, and create forms that are used for gathering information from the user.

The standard way to type tags is in ALL CAPS. However, most browsers will work with tags typed in ALL CAPS or lower case or a Mix Of The Two. I have used all caps in this book.

Some tags can be used by themselves, like **<P>**, the tag that starts a paragraph. Other tags must be used together; for example, to style a first level heading requires opening and closing tags, **<H1>** and **</H1>**. Closing tags contain a slash. Tags for linking files and creating forms require additional parts (also called *arguments*) to work properly. Tags for graphics also require additional parts like the file name and directions for alignment.

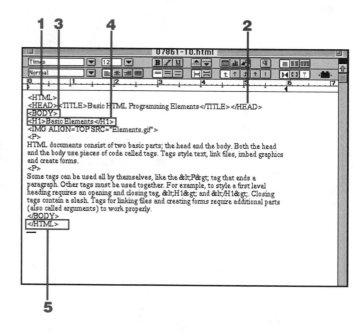

1 Each document should start with the <HTML> tag. If you are using an HTML editor, the files may not include this tag.

2 The <HEAD> tag must be at the beginning of your document. Put the <TITLE> tag between the <HEAD> and </HEAD> tags which surround the prologue of the file. Type the text you want to appear in the title bar of the browser when the file is viewed between the <TITLE> and </TITLE> tags.

3 Place the rest of your document between the <BODY> and </BODY> tags.

4 The <H1> and </H1> tags surround the text that appears in the first level heading style.

5 End every document with </HTML>.

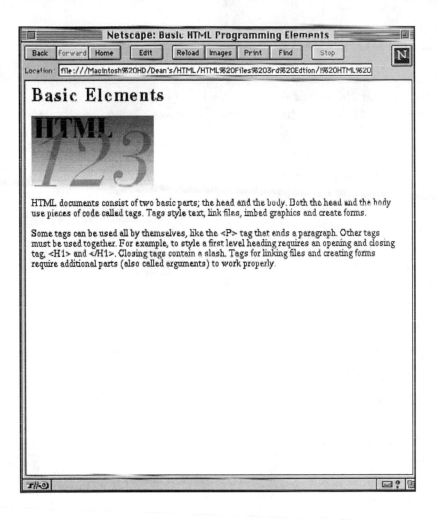

Netscape: Basic HTML Programming Elements

| Back | Forward | Home | | Edit | | Reload | Images | Print | Find | | Stop | |

Location: file:///Macintosh%20HD/Dean's/HTML/HTML%20Files%203rd%20Edtion/!%20HTML%20

Basic Elements

HTML documents consist of two basic parts; the head and the body. Both the head and the body use pieces of code called tags. Tags style text, link files, imbed graphics and create forms.

Some tags can be used all by themselves, like the <P> tag that ends a paragraph. Other tags must be used together. For example, to style a first level heading requires an opening and closing tag, <H1> and </H1>. Closing tags contain a slash. Tags for linking files and creating forms require additional parts (also called arguments) to work properly.

Relative Type Styles

One way to style type is with *relative tags*. These include six heading tags (H1 through H6) and tags like *strong* and *emphasis*. Each tag indicates a style set in the browser preferences. Styles vary from browser to browser but generally have the same characteristics (see page 10).

Heading styles H1 through H6 start large and bold and gradually lessen in size and weight. H5 and H6 style preferences can be very different from those in the browser you use. You may get a result you don't like, so it is a good idea to stay away from them.

H1 is the largest and boldest; use it for the most important type on your page. H2 is smaller and less bold; use it for sub-heads. H3 is smaller and carries less weight than H1 or H2; use it when you need to have a third level of heading. Use H4, H5, and H6 sparingly. You do not want your page to look like an out-line (unless, of course, it is).

Address is often italic and is meant for e-mail, phone numbers, and postal addresses. The tag for address is **<ADDRESS>**.

Citation is meant for quoting text, and its tag is **<CITE>**.

Emphasis and *strong* draw the eye to the type, usually by making it bold or italic. These are marked with the **<EM>** and **<STRONG>** tags.

Code, sample and *keyboard* format type in a monospaced font, usually Courier. These are marked with the **<CODE>**, **<SAMP>**, and **<KBD>** tags.

Other relative tags include **<BIG>**; **<SMALL>**; **<SUP>**, for superscripts; and **<SUB>** for subscripts.

If you do not indicate a type style, the text is formatted in plain type. All of these type-style tags are used in pairs. The closing tags for heading styles insert a paragraph break automatically. Other text styles, often used within copy, do not.

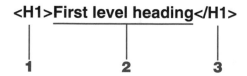

<H1>First level heading</H1>

1   2   3

1   Start with an opening tag in front of the text.

2   Put the text you want to style between the tags.

3   End with a closing tag after the text.

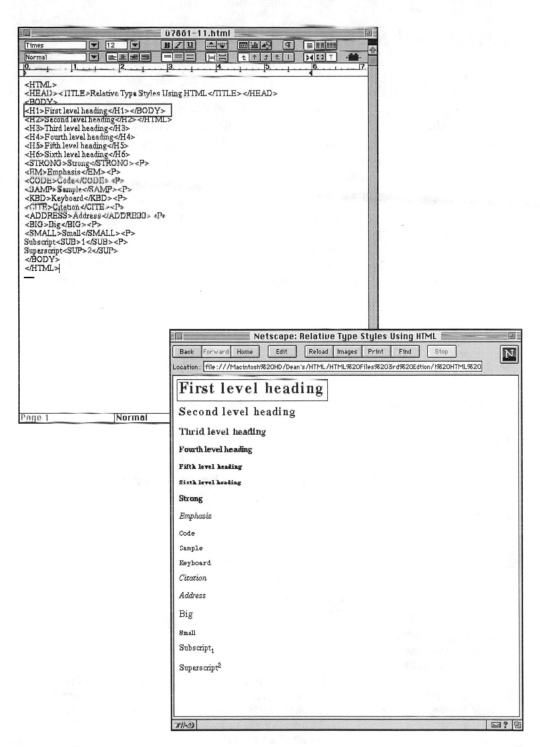

Horizontal Alignment of Text and Graphics

You can control horizontal alignment of text and graphics through HTML programming. Unless you specify alignment, all elements in a document will align left and have a ragged right margin. This looks fine for many documents. However, you may want to design a more distinctive page by choosing left, right, or centered alignment.

Long paragraphs of centered copy can be difficult to read, but centering adds a certain look that may fit the character of the Web pages you design.

Some browsers also support **<Left>** and **<Right>** tags that work the same way as **<Center>**. However, more recent releases of browser software recognize **Align=** instead of **<Left>** and **<Right>**. Use **Align=** inside paragraph, **<P>**, and heading tags, **<H1>**.

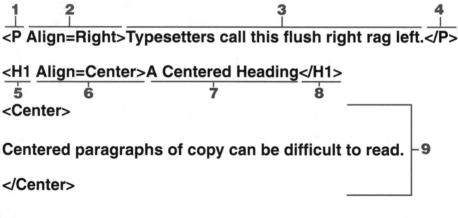

<P Align=Right>Typesetters call this flush right rag left.</P>

<H1 Align=Center>A Centered Heading</H1>

<Center>

Centered paragraphs of copy can be difficult to read.

</Center>

1 Start with the <P tag in front of the text.

2 Put the Align argument after the <P tag. Put the alignment option after the = symbol and close the tag with the > symbol.

3 Put text, graphics, and other elements between the tags.

4 End with a closing tag to return to default alignment.

5 Start with any heading style tag in front of the text. This will also add a line space.

6 Put the Align argument after the heading style tag. Put the alignment option after the = symbol and close the tag with the > symbol.

7 Put text, graphics, and other elements between the tags.

8 End with a closing tag to return to default alignment and text style.

9 Put text, graphics, and other HTML elements between the <Center> and </Center> tags.

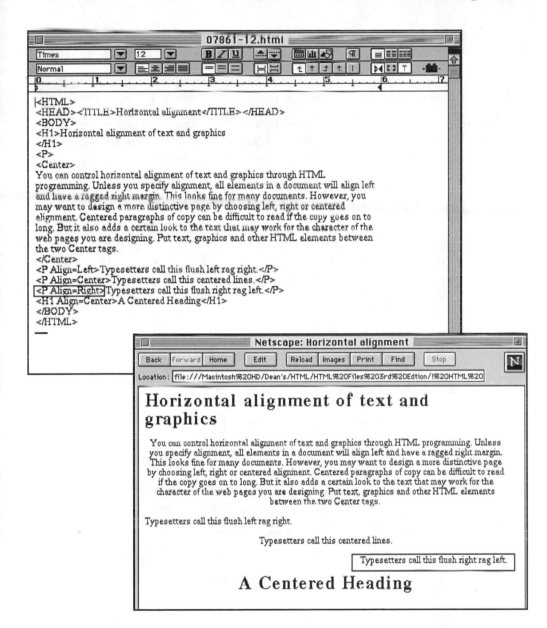

Font Sizes

One way to change text size displayed by the browser is by using heading styles (see page 22). Another way is by setting the basefont size or the font size.

<Basefont> affects the default size used for text. Heading styles override basefont size. The default basefont size is 3 unless you specify a different one. This is very readable for most documents. Basefont sizes range from 1 to 7.

<Font> affects the size used for specific pieces of text. Heading styles override font size. Font sizes range from 1 to 7. Setting the font size and basefont size to the same number result in the same size type.

Setting the font size with a + or - symbol results in sizes relative to the current basefont size. You cannot have the font and basefont size add up to more than 7 or less than 1. For example, if the basefont size is set at 3, you can only add 4 or subtract 2 using font size.

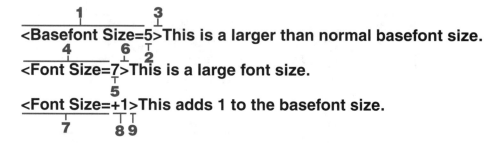

1 **Start with the** <Basefont Size = **tag.**

2 **Put the size after the** = **symbol. Set it from 1 to 7.**

3 **Close the tag with the** > **symbol.**

4 **Start with the** <Font Size= **tag.**

5 **Put the size after the** = **symbol. Set it from 1 to 7.**

6 **Close the tag with the** > **symbol.**

7 **Start with the** <Font Size= **tag.**

8 **Put the relative size after the** = **symbol.**

9 **Close the tag with the** > **symbol.**

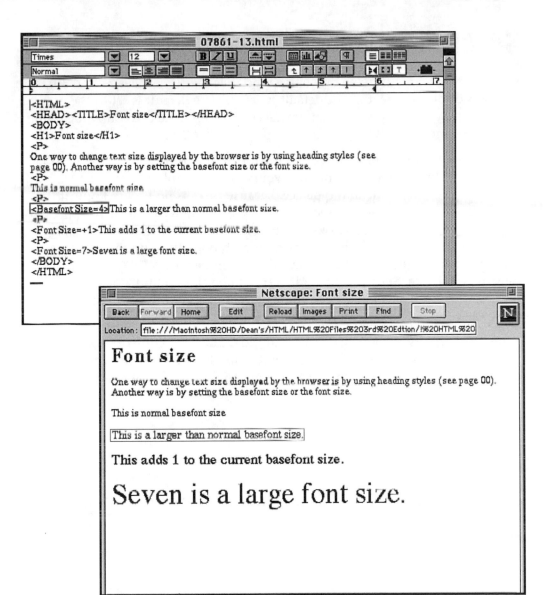

Specifying Typefaces and Color

When styling text with fixed or relative type style tags (see pages 22 and 30), browsers display the text in the default typeface. The default is set in the user preferences. You can specify other typefaces and control text color by including the **FACE=** and **COLOR=** arguments within the **<FONT** tag.

There is one big problem when specifying fonts. The fonts you choose must be installed on the user's system, not just yours. If they aren't, the browser will still display the text in the default typeface. Because there is no way to know if the fonts are available on the user's system, you have a choice of just two approaches. You can either choose one typeface that is standard across most operating systems or you can specify one typeface for each operating system by listing several typefaces, separated by commas. For example, **<FONT FACE="Arial**, **Helvetica**, **Geneva**, **Swiss**, **Sans Serif**"**>** should be able to find at least one of these san serif fonts installed on most Windows or Macintosh systems. The browser uses the first font it finds installed.

You set text colors in the **<FONT** tag with the **COLOR=** argument. Color is a mix of red, green, and blue in hexadecimal notation. Black is 000000—that is, no color. White is ffffff, or full color. Experiment to find combinations you like. You also can specify color by name instead of number. Common colors like green, yellow, and red have been given numeric equivalents (see page 200).

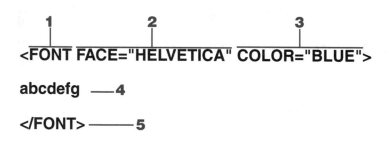

1 Start with the <FONT **tag.**

2 Include the FACE= argument within the <FONT **tag if you want to specify a typeface. Put the name of the typeface between the quote marks.**

3 Include the COLOR= argument within the <FONT **tag if you want to specify a color. Put the name of the color or the hexadecimal notation between the quote marks.**

4 Put all the text between the opening <FONT> **tag and the closing** </FONT> **tag.**

5 End with the closing </FONT> **tag to return to the default text style.**

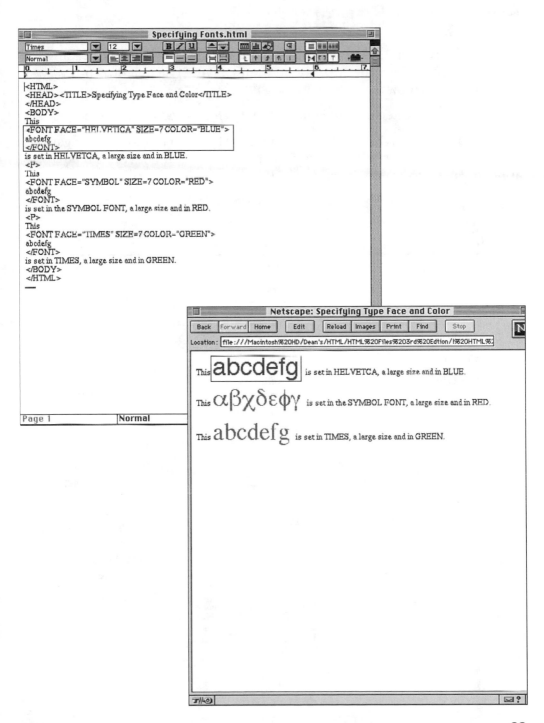

Fixed Type Styles

One way to style type is with *fixed tags*. Unlike relative style tags for heading levels or emphasis, each of these tags indicates a type style that does not vary from browser to browser.

If you do not indicate any type style, the text is formatted in plain type.

Blink is an unusual style. It makes text alternate between positive and negative. Black text becomes white text on a strip of black background. This can be annoying but effective in drawing attention to specific elements.

The various fixed type styles and their tags are:

Style	Tag
Bold	<B>
Italic	<I>
Underscore	<U>
Typewriter	<TT>
Strikeout	<S>
Blink (Navigator only)	<BLINK>

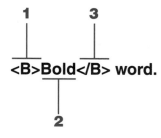

1 Start with an opening tag in front of the text.

2 Put the text you want to style between the tags.

3 End with a closing tag after the text.

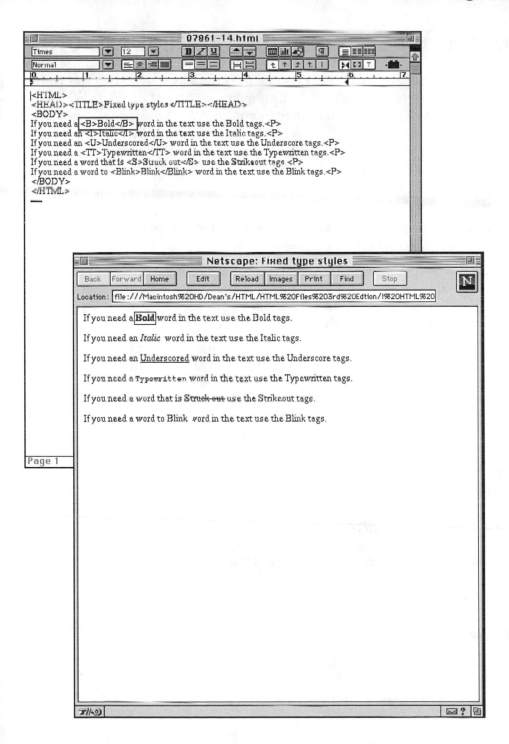

```
<HTML>
<HEAD><TITLE>Fixed type styles </TITLE></HEAD>
<BODY>
If you need a <B>Bold</B> word in the text use the Bold tags.<P>
If you need an <I>Italic</I> word in the text use the Italic tags.<P>
If you need an <U>Underscored</U> word in the text use the Underscore tags.<P>
If you need a <TT>Typewritten</TT> word in the text use the Typewritten tags.<P>
If you need a word that is <S>Struck out</S> use the Strikeout tags <P>
If you need a word to <Blink>Blink</Blink> word in the text use the Blink tags.<P>
</BODY>
</HTML>
```

Netscape: Fixed type styles

Back Forward Home   Edit   Reload Images Print Find   Stop

Location: file:///Macintosh%20HD/Dean's/HTML/HTML%20Files%203rd%20Edtion/!%20HTML%20

If you need a **Bold** word in the text use the Bold tags.

If you need an *Italic* word in the text use the Italic tags.

If you need an Underscored word in the text use the Underscore tags.

If you need a Typewritten word in the text use the Typewritten tags.

If you need a word that is Struck out use the Strikeout tags.

If you need a word to Blink word in the text use the Blink tags.

Setting Type Styles with Internet Explorer

Until the introduction of the **<STYLE>** tag, the only way to style text was with relative or fixed styles (see pages 22-30). Paired tags, like **<H1>** and **</H1>** or **<B>** and **</B>**, surround the text and change its appearance. Font size, face, and color can also alter the look of text. However, this requires repeatedly typing a lot of code throughout the file when complex styles are used alternately. Setting a type style, also called a style sheet, with the **<STYLE>** tag is an easier way to do this.

The **<STYLE>** tag is not yet fully adopted by any browser. Many do not support it at all. The explanation below covers the two most basic ways of using the **<STYLE>** tag with Internet Explorer. Future plans call for greatly expanding this extension of the official HTML language.

Setting a type style is, essentially, modifying a heading style. In other words, you modify any of the preset styles **<H1>** through **<H6>** with the **<STYLE>** tag. Redefine **<H1>** once in the **<HEAD>** of the file and the new **<H1>** style is available just by using the paired **<H1>** and **</H1>** tags.

You can also set a style within a heading tag by using the **STYLE=** argument. This is useful if you want to change the heading style for one instance only. This will effect the style of the text surrounded by that particular set of paired tags. It will not change the overall heading style for the rest of the document.

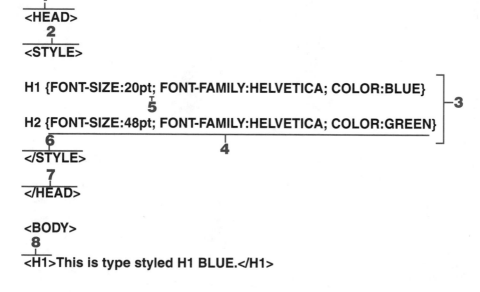

```
       1
    ‾‾‾|‾‾‾
    <HEAD>
       2
    ‾‾‾|‾‾‾
    <STYLE>


    H1 {FONT-SIZE:20pt; FONT-FAMILY:HELVETICA; COLOR:BLUE} ⎤
                    5                                       ⎥─3
    H2 {FONT-SIZE:48pt; FONT-FAMILY:HELVETICA; COLOR:GREEN} ⎦
       6                              4
    ‾‾‾|‾‾‾
    </STYLE>
       7
    ‾‾‾|‾‾‾
    </HEAD>


    <BODY>
       8
    ‾‾‾|‾‾‾
    <H1>This is type styled H1 BLUE.</H1>
```

10

<H1 STYLE="FONT-SIZE:48pt; FONT-FAMILY:TIMES; COLOR:ORANGE"> 9

This is type styled H1 ORANGE.</H1>
11

1 Start with the <HEAD> tag at the beginning of the file.

2 Put the <STYLE> tags between the <HEAD> tags to define a type style.

3 Put the heading style you want to redefine between the paired style tags.

4 Put the font attributes between curly brackets.

5 Separate each attribute with a semicolon.

6 Close the style with the </STYLE> tag.

7 Close the head with the </HEAD> tag.

8 Use the redefined heading tag in the body of the file.

9 If you want to change a heading style just once, include the STYLE= argument within the heading tag when used in the body of the file.

10 Put all the type attributes between quote marks after the STYLE= argument.

11 Put the text between the paired heading tags.

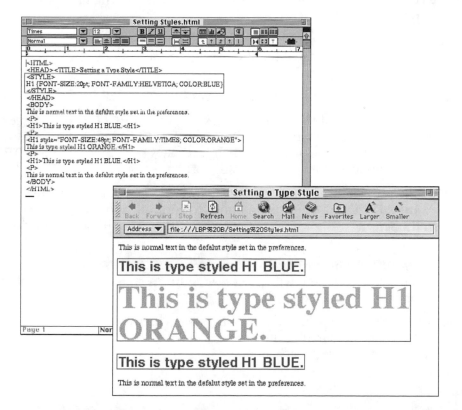

Marquees for Internet Explorer

Internet Explorer has a unique HTML tag for making text move across the screen: the **<MARQUEE>** tag. Any text within this tag will attract the viewer's attention by scrolling across the screen. As with **<BLINK>** (see page 30), it can be annoying if used too often.

You control various marquee characteristics with the arguments to the **<MARQUEE>** tag, which are explained below. Experiment to find a balance between the length of message, size of type, and marquee speed so that the marquee is readable—not so slow that it becomes tiresome and not so fast that it is too hard to read as it zips past.

HEIGHT= controls the height of the marquee, which is measured in pixels.

WIDTH= controls the width of the marquee, which is measured in pixels or by percent of window size.

HSPACE= and **VSPACE=** control the horizontal and vertical spaces between the text within the marquee and the edge of the marquee. **HSPACE=** and **VSPACE=** are measured in pixels.

ALIGN= controls where the text appears in relationship to the marquee. Choose between **TOP**, **MIDDLE**, or **BOTTOM**.

BGCOLOR= enables you to set the background color. Color is a mix of red, green, and blue in hexadecimal notation. You also can specify color by name instead of number (see page 28).

DIRECTION= controls whether the text moves **RIGHT** or **LEFT**.

BEHAVIOR= controls just that—how the text moves. **SCROLL** makes the text enter from one side of the screen and exit the other. **SLIDE** makes the text enter from one side of the screen and stop when it reaches the other. **ALTERNATE** makes the text bounce from one side to the other.

LOOP= controls the number of times the text moves across the marquee. Use the word **INFINITE** if you want the marquee to continue looping as long as the file is on the screen. **LOOP=** does not effect **SLIDE** or **ALTERNATE** behaviors.

SCROLLAMOUNT= controls how far the text steps each time it moves. **SCROLLAMOUNT** is measured in pixels. A large **SCROLLAMOUNT** will cause the text to move in jerks and will affect readability. A small **SCROLLAMOUNT** will slow down the movement.

SCROLLDELAY= controls how long the text waits between steps. **SCROLLDELAY** is measured in thousandths of seconds. A **SCROLLDELAY=1000** pauses one second between each step.

1

<MARQUEE

2

HEIGHT=50 WIDTH=75%

HSPACE=5 VSPACE=5

ALIGN=TOP

BGCOLOR=Yellow

3

DIRECTION=LEFT LOOP=INFINITE BEHAVIOR=SCROLL

SCROLLAMOUNT=5 SCROLLDELAY=100>

This message will scroll from left to right across the screen.— 4

</MARQUEE>—5

1 Start with the <MARQUEE tag.

2 Define the HEIGHT= and WIDTH= of the marquee. Height and width are measured in pixels or as a percent of window width.

3 Define all other marquee characteristics you choose to control. See explanations above.

4 Put the scrolling text between the opening <MARQUEE> and closing </MARQUEE> tags.

5 End with the closing </MARQUEE> tag.

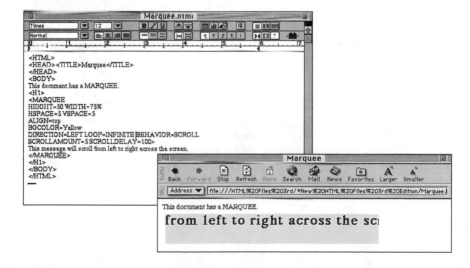

Line and Paragraph Breaks

The line break tag, **
, ends a line whether following text or graphics. The paragraph break tag, **<P>, ends a line and inserts a line space that separates elements visually. Both tags are used alone, not in pairs like the **<B>** and **</B>** tags.

You must insert a tag when you want to break a line or end a paragraph in a specific place. Otherwise, the text flows to fit the width of the browser window and breaks differently when the browser window is resized.

The **<NoBR>** tag prevents text and graphics from breaking and reflowing to fit the browser window. It is a paired tag. If you want to indicate a place to break text within non-breaking sections, use **<WBR>**. Place this tag within the **<NoBR>** and **</NoBR>** tags.

There are plenty of other good reasons to break lines and paragraphs. Breaking large copy blocks into smaller concise segments helps readability. Obviously, you want to break lines of poetry and address blocks. To break text wrapping around graphics so that text starts below the image, use the **<BR Clear=** tag (see page 40).

**There are plenty of good reasons to break
**

**lines
** ——————— **1**

**and
**

paragraphs.

<P> ——————— **2**

Breaking large copy into smaller concise segments helps readability. Obviously, you will want to break lines of poetry and address blocks.

<P>
<NoBR> ——————— **3**

The no break tag prevents text and graphics from reflowing to fit the browser window. It is a paired tag. <WBR> If you want to indicate a place to break text within non-breaking sections, use word break tag. Place this tag within the no break tags. **4**

</NoBR>

1
 ends a line without adding any space.

2 <P> **ends a paragraph and adds a line space.**

3 **Put** <NoBR> **and** </NoBR> **around sections that should not break.**

4 **Put** <WBR> **inside the no break tags to indicate where to break if needed.**

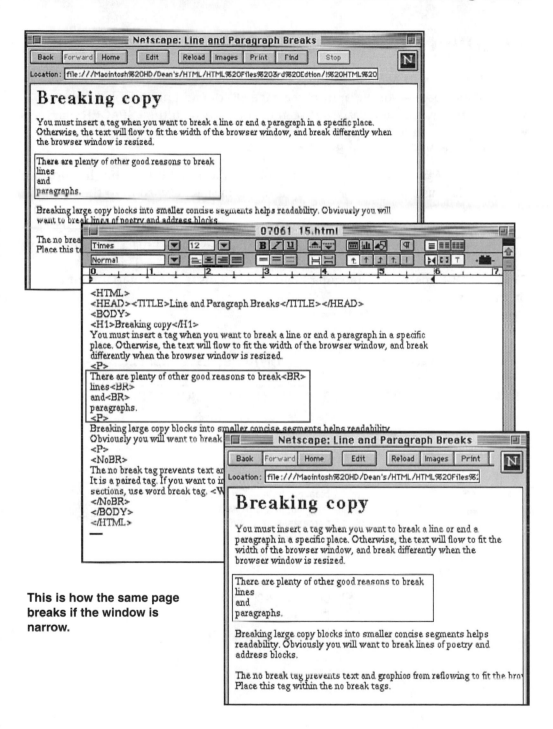

This is how the same page breaks if the window is narrow.

Adding Space in Netscape

Some HTML tags allow you to add space around text or graphics. For instance, you can add space around graphics (see page 68) or padding in tables (see page 128). Another way to add space between elements is with the **<SPACER>** tag, which enables you to add space in three ways by defining the type of spacer as **HORIZONTAL**, **VERTICAL**, or **BLOCK**.

The spacer **TYPE=HORIZONTAL** inserts a blank space that is wide but has no height. This is useful because HTML ignores extra spaces typed in to the text, unless it is preformatted (see page 82). This is an easy way to add space between letters or words. The spacer **TYPE=VERTICAL** inserts a line space of an exact height. Horizontal and vertical spacers are also a way to add space on one side of a graphic but not the other, or above a graphic but not below. The spacer **TYPE=BLOCK** inserts a rectangular blank space. This is one way to indent text or graphics.

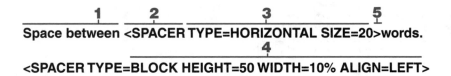

Space between <SPACER TYPE=HORIZONTAL SIZE=20>words.

<SPACER TYPE=BLOCK HEIGHT=50 WIDTH=10% ALIGN=LEFT>

1 Start with the text.

2 Insert the <SPACER tag.

3 Choose HORIZONTAL, VERTICAL, or BLOCK as the TYPE= of space and include the size, measured in pixels.

4 For BLOCK spaces, include the size of the HEIGHT and WIDTH. Measure both HEIGHT and WIDTH in pixels or as a percentage of window size. Also include the ALIGN= tag. Choose between LEFT or RIGHT.

5 Close the SPACER tag with the > symbol.

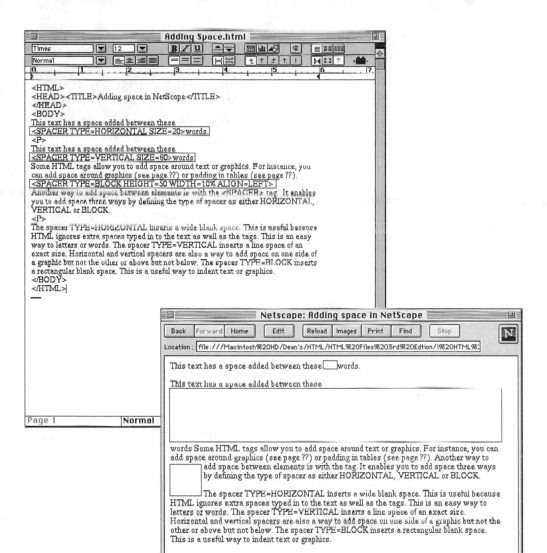

Clearing Text Wrap

You wrap text around graphics with the **<IMG Align=** tag (see page 66). Text wraps around the graphic until reaching the bottom of the graphic. However, you may want to stop text wrapping before it reaches the bottom to improve design and readability.

Use the **<BR Clear=** tag to break lines and end wrapping. This tag causes copy to start on the next free line below the graphic. There are three options. **Clear=right** starts copy on the next free line on the right margin. **Clear=left** starts copy on the next free line on the left margin. **Clear=all** starts copy on the next free line on both right and left margins.

1

<IMG SRC="Clips1.gif" Align=left>

This copy will continue to wrap around the graphic and then break here.

2   3

<BR Clear=left>

4

Then the copy will continue on the next free left margin, running on just like any other text on the screen.

1 Insert the graphic using the <IMG SRC= tag and choose an alignment option (see pages 64 and 66).

2 Put the <BR tag after the text you want to break.

3 Put Clear= followed by the margin option. Choose between right, left, and all.

4 Close the tag with the > symbol.

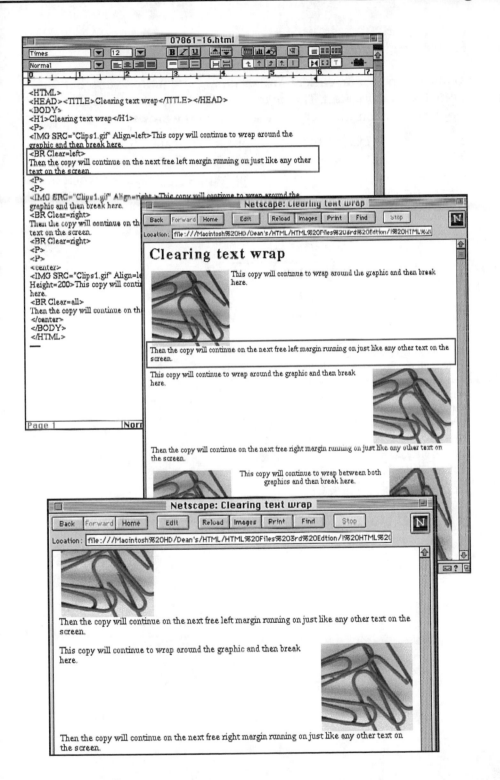

Text Links

Linked text allows a person to click a word or phrase and jump to another file. This capability is called *hypertext*. The linked text shows up in color and is underscored depending on the preference settings of the browser.

Type the example below exactly the way it appears to create a link to a file named Art.html. To make your own linked text, just substitute the file name and the copy that gets clicked to whatever you want. Page 58 shows when to use just a file name and when to use a full path.

1 Start with the opening tag <A HREF= in front of the file name. Think of the <A as meaning anchor and HREF as meaning hypertext reference.

2 Put the file name you want to link between the quote marks.

3 Put the text you want people to click on the screen between the > and < symbols.

4 End with a closing tag </A> after the text.

42

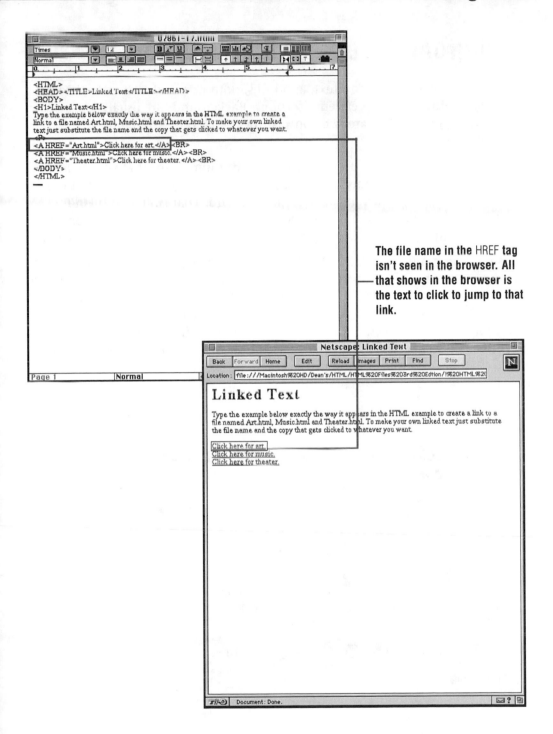

The file name in the HREF tag isn't seen in the browser. All that shows in the browser is the text to click to jump to that link.

Background, Text, and Link Colors

Browsers display backgrounds, text, and links, both new and visited, in default colors determined by the preference settings. Backgrounds are usually gray or white. Text is black. Links are two contrasting colors so they pop out of unlinked text.

Since color preferences vary from user to user, it is important that you set all these colors in every document you create. If you don't, your file may not look the way you expect. In fact, it can look pretty weird. That isn't a problem for uninhibited cybermaniacs. It is a problem for designers maintaining an online corporate identity.

You set background, text, and link colors in the body tag at the beginning of an HTML file. Color is a mix of red, green, and blue in hexadecimal notation. Black is 000000—that is, no color. White is ffffff, or full color. Experiment to find the combinations you like. You can also specify color by name instead of number. Common colors like green, yellow, and red have been given numeric equivalents (see page 200). Remember, transparent graphics designed for white backgrounds won't look good on dark colors.

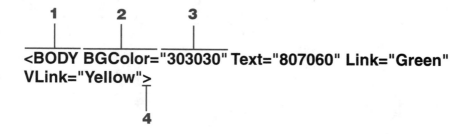

```
1       2       3
|       |       |
<BODY BGColor="303030" Text="807060" Link="Green"
VLink="Yellow">
          |
          4
```

1 Start with the <BODY tag.

2 Put BGColor=, Text=, Link=, and VLink= after the opening <BODY tag. Think of BGColor as meaning background color and VLink as visited link.

3 Put the values of red, green, and blue, or the color name, between quotes for each.

4 Close the tag with the > symbol.

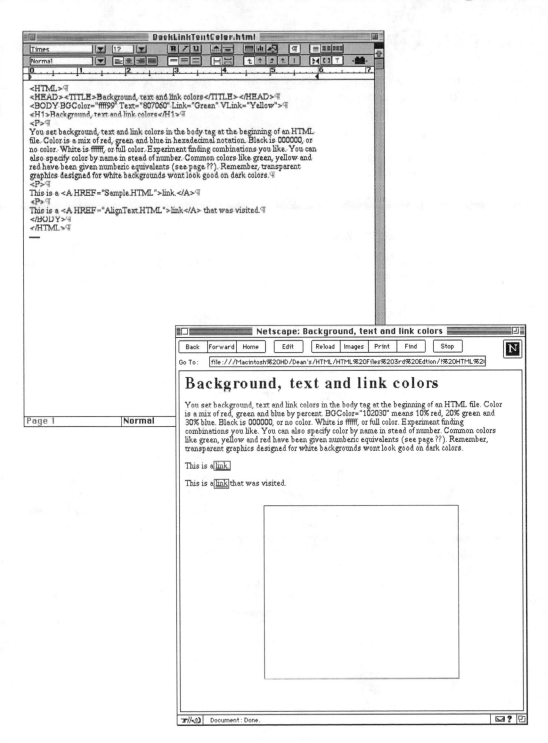

Graphic Links

Linked graphics allow a person to click an image and jump to another file. This capability can make your documents easier to use. Good clear graphics communicate quickly and enhance the usability of your document. The linked graphic shows up outlined in color depending on the preference settings of the browser.

To link a graphic, type the same code as for linked text. In place of the clickable text, insert a graphic for users to click.

Type the example below exactly the way it appears to create a link to a file named Art.html. To make your own linked graphic, just substitute the file name and the image that gets clicked with your own file name and image.

For other ways to create links with graphics, see Image Maps—Using CGI Scripts (page 90), Image Maps—Using Browsers (page 92), and Graphic Send Buttons (page 116).

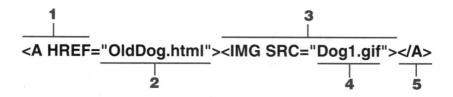

1 Start with the opening tag `<A HREF=` in front of the file name.

2 Put the file name you want to link between the quote marks.

3 Put the `<IMG>` tag (the tag that inserts a graphic on the screen, see page 64) between the `>` and `<` symbols of the link tag. Think of IMG as meaning image.

4 Put the file name of the image you want people to click between the quote marks of the `<IMG>` tag.

5 End with a closing tag `</A>` for the link after the last part of the `<IMG>` tag.

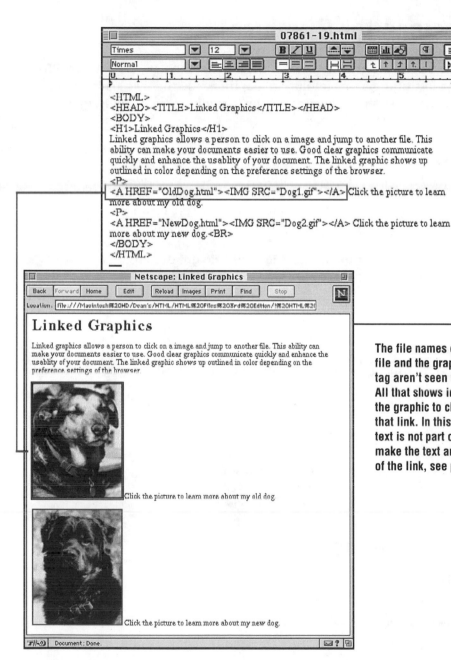

The file names of the linked file and the graphic in the HRFF tag aren't seen in the browser. All that shows in the browser is the graphic to click to jump to that link. In this example, the text is not part of the link. To make the text and graphic part of the link, see page 56.

Dimensions for Graphics

The time it takes to load graphics is one problem of Web page design. **LowSRC** can help by substituting a low resolution graphic while the text loads (see page 64). Another way to speed up load time is by including **Width** and **Height** dimensions as part of the **<IMG** tag.

Width and **Height** dimensions, which are measured in pixels, tell the browser how large an image will be without retrieving the entire graphic file. With the dimensions, the browser first blocks out the required space, lays out the document, displays the text, and then loads the graphic. This means the person viewing your page will have something to read while the images load.

Scaling graphics is another use of the **Width** and **Height** dimensions. Browsers will stretch or squeeze graphics to fit the size you define.

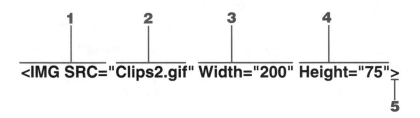

1 Start with the opening tag <IMG SRC= **in front of the file name. Think of** SRC **as meaning source.**

2 Put the graphic file name you want displayed between the quote marks.

3 Put Width= **followed by the dimension measured in pixels within the** <IMG **tag.**

4 Put Height= **followed by the dimension measured in pixels within the** <IMG **tag.**

5 End with a closing tag >.

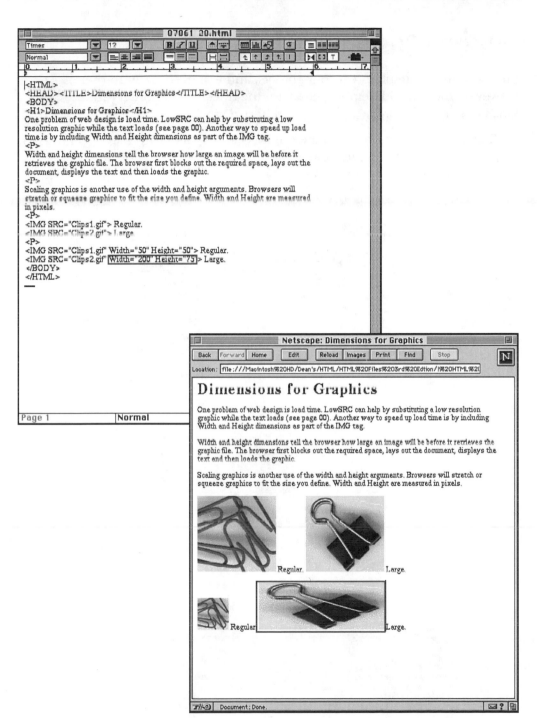

Borders on Graphic Links

Browsers display graphics without borders, and graphic links with them. However, you can add, remove, and vary the thickness of borders around both kinds of graphics. Borders are measured in pixels.

Adding borders to graphics that are not links and eliminating them from linked graphics can confuse people viewing your file because this is contrary to the standard way of identifying links.

1 **2**

<IMG SRC="Dog1.gif" Border=12>

3

1 Start with the <IMG SRC tag in front of the file name (see page 64).

2 Put Border= after the file name and the width of the border measured in pixels after the = symbol.

3 Close the tag with the > symbol.

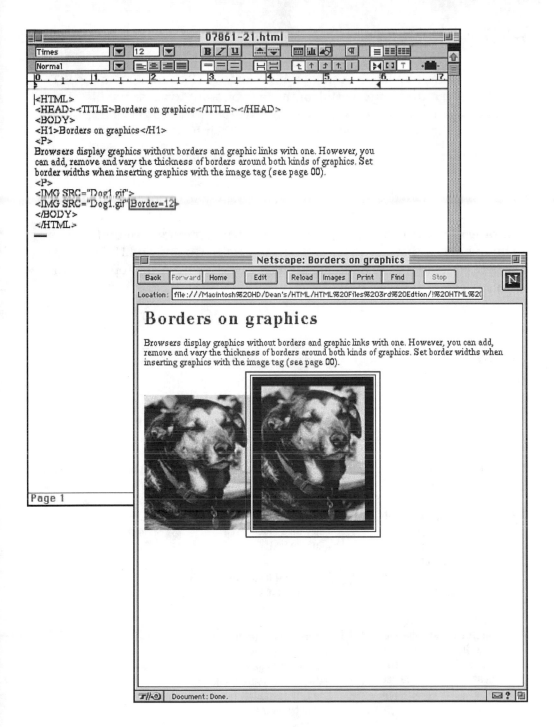

FTP and E-Mail

Browsers can retrieve files by using an anonymous FTP to connect to the FTP servers. Just put the complete URL of the file you want to get as the file name of the link. When someone clicks the link for the file in their browser, the browser connects to the FTP server and saves the file to their hard disk.

Some browsers also send e-mail. Put the complete e-mail address as the file name of a link. When a person clicks the link, a dialog box appears for the subject and body of the message.

The format for the address that you link to uses URLs. The URL includes the type of service, the address, the path, and the file name. You can use this same technique shown here for FTP servers to connect to Gopher and UseNet news. The URL codes for the most popular Internet services are at the top of the following page.

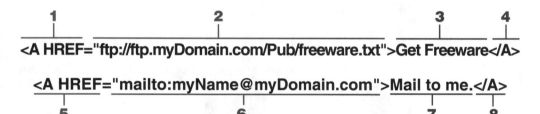

```
1                        2                                    3        4
<A HREF="ftp://ftp.myDomain.com/Pub/freeware.txt">Get Freeware</A>

    <A HREF="mailto:myName@myDomain.com">Mail to me.</A>
        5                        6                    7        8
```

1 Start with the opening tag in front of the URL.

2 Put the complete URL of the file you want to retrieve between the quote marks. This includes the URL code for FTP (ftp://), the address of the FTP server (ftp.myDomain.com), the path (/Pub/), and the file name (freeware.txt). FTP paths and file names can be case sensitive, so use the correct capitalization.

3 Put the text you want people to click between the > and < symbols.

4 End with a closing tag after the text.

5 Start with the opening tag in front of the e-mail address.

6 Put the complete URL of the person you want to send a message to between the quote marks. The URL is mailto: followed by their e-mail address.

7 Put the text you want people to click between the > and < symbols.

8 End with a closing tag after the text.

Internet Service	URL Code
World Wide Web	http://
FTP	ftp://
Gopher	gopher://
Mail	mailto: (Not all browsers support this.)
UseNet News	news:

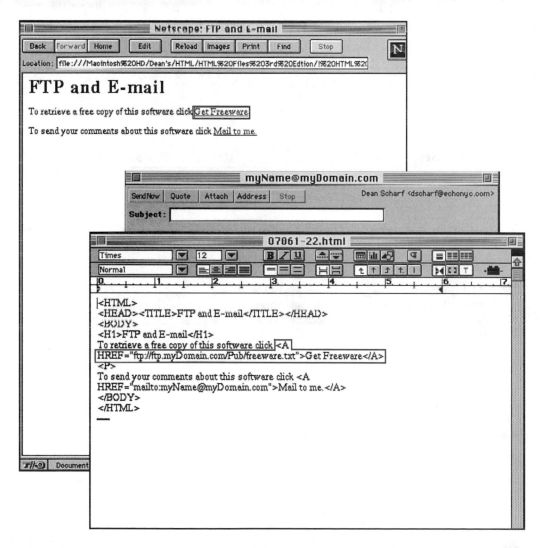

Alternatives to Images for Non-Graphical Browsers

People using non-graphical browsers, like Lynx, and people who turn off the image loading in graphical browsers do not see in-line graphics on their screens. They only see text; the word **[IMAGE]** replaces the graphic. If you want them to know what graphic you inserted, you have a problem.

The solution is an extended version of the **<IMG>** tag. The **<ALT>** tag allows you to include a description of the graphic. This descriptive copy substitutes for the graphic. It is a good idea to do this for all graphics.

Another alternative here is to simply include a separate text link following the graphic link for any picture. That way, people using browsers that don't support the **<ALT>** tag still have a link to use.

1   **3**   **5**

<IMG SRC="Dog1.gif" ALT="[Picture of a mixed breed.]">

2   **4**

1 Start with the opening tag <IMG SRC= in front of the graphic file name.

2 Put the graphic file name between the quote marks.

3 Put the <ALT> tag after the name of the graphic file.

4 Put the descriptive copy that substitutes for the graphic between the brackets of the <ALT> tag.

5 End with a closing > symbol of the <IMG> tag.

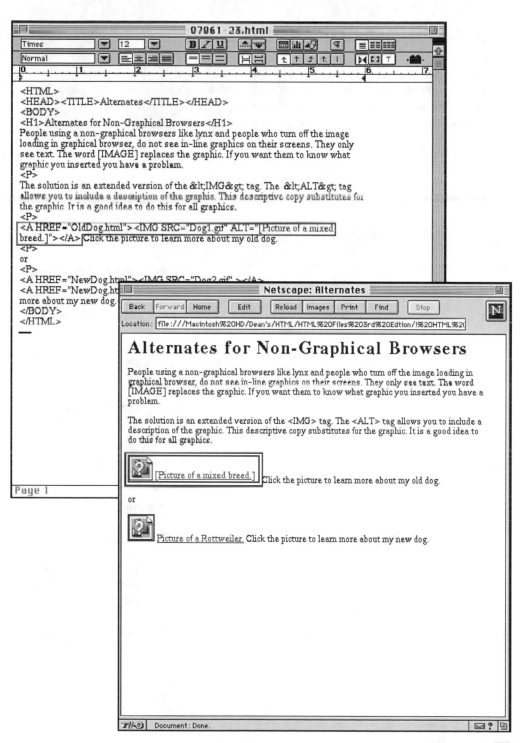

Links Within Documents

Text and graphics can link to places within the same document. These links require two parts: the anchor and the link. The *anchor* identifies the place to jump to. The *link* uses the name of the anchor instead of the name of a file. (The list items used in the example code here are explained on pages 52–53.)

Link

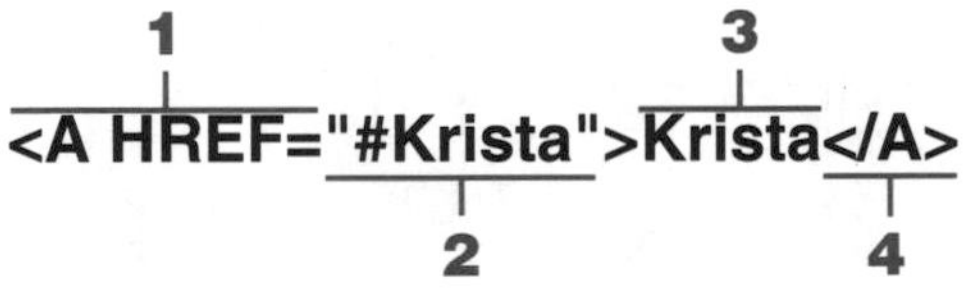

1	Start with the opening tag <A HREF= in front of the anchor name.
2	Put a # symbol followed by the anchor name you want to link to between the quote marks.
3	Put the text you want people to click on between the > and < symbols.
4	End with a closing tag </A> after the text.

Anchor

5	Start with the opening tag <A NAME= in front of the anchor name.
6	Put the name of the anchor between the quote marks.
7	Put the text that appears on the screen between the > and < symbols.
8	End with a closing tag </A> behind the text.

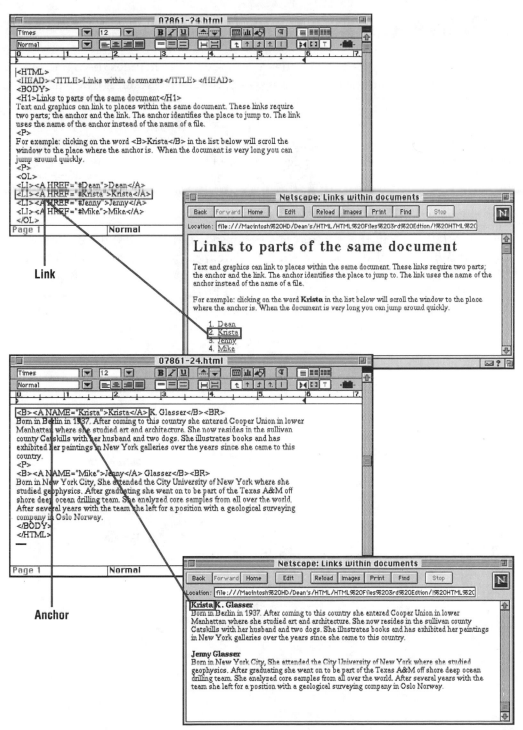

Link

Anchor

Relative and Absolute Path Names

An URL describes the location of a file. A complete URL includes the name of the server, disk, and all the directories within which a file resides. URLs are also called *paths*. There are two types of paths.

Absolute paths spell out the location of a file by starting at the highest level and listing each directory needed to find the file. You start the path with the type of service, which is http:// for Web pages, followed by the name of the server, a slash (/), and the exact name of each directory and the file. Getting one part of the URL wrong means the file won't be found. You will have to change paths in your document if a disk or directory name changes.

Relative paths spell out the location of a file based on the current document location. When you use a file name like xyzFile.html, you are using a relative URL. In this case, the browser looks for the file in the same directory as the current document. If it is not there, the file won't be found. When you type **../** in front of the file name (i.e., ../xyzFile.html), the browser looks for the file in the directory one level above the current document. When you type **../../** in front of the file name (i.e., ../../xyzFile.html), the browser looks for the file in the directory two levels above the current document.

Web URLs are case sensitive, so be sure to use proper capitalization.

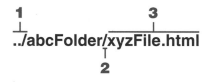

1 Using **../** indicates a directory level above the current directory.

2 The directory names are separated by slashes.

3 The file name.

URL	Where the referenced file is found
xyzFile.html	The HTML file named xyzFile.html is found in the current directory
abcFolder/xyzFile.html	The HTML file named xyzFile.html is found in the folder named abcFolder in the current directory
http://myDomain.com /abcFolder/xyzFile.html	The HTML file named xyzFile.html is found in the folder named abcFolder on the server named myDomain.com
../abcFolder/xyzFile.html	The HTML file named xyzFile.html is found in the folder named abcFolder one directory level above the current directory
../../abcFolder/xyzFile.html	The HTML file named xyzFile.html is found in the folder named abcFolder two directory levels above the current directory

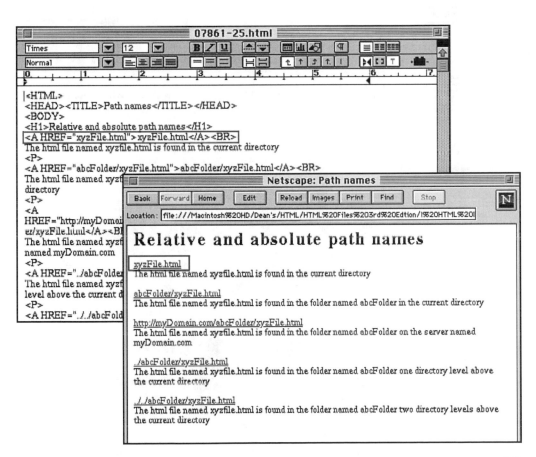

Block Quotes

One way to style type so that it stands out from the rest of your copy is by using the **<BLOCKQUOTE>** tag. This tag indents the text. You still have to use the **<P>** and **
** tags to break paragraphs and lines in particular places (see page 36).

<BLOCKQUOTE>————————**1**

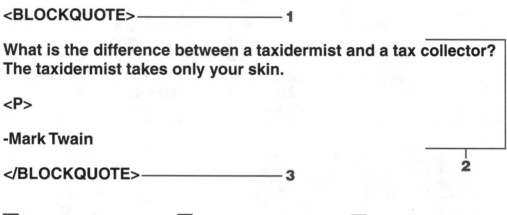

What is the difference between a taxidermist and a tax collector? The taxidermist takes only your skin.

<P>

-Mark Twain

2

</BLOCKQUOTE>————————**3**

1 Start with an opening tag in front of the text.

2 Put the text you want to style between the tags.

3 End with a closing tag after the text.

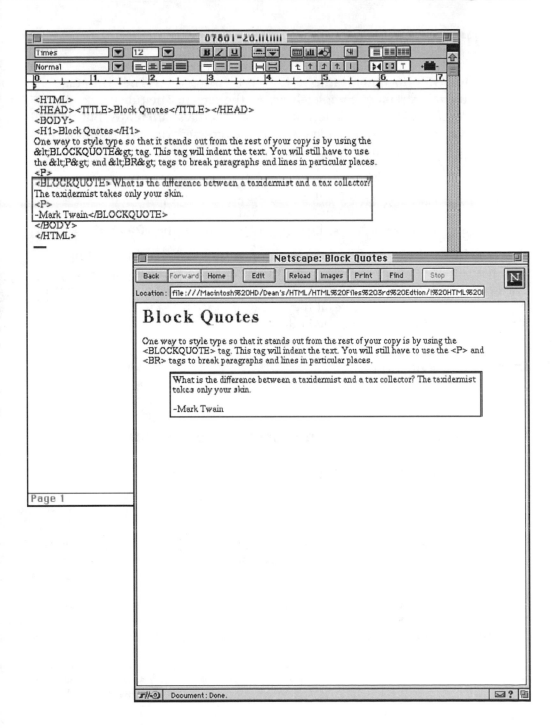

Dividing Rules

One way to divide documents into sections is by using rules. The **<HR>** tag inserts a rule that stretches completely across the screen. The rule breaks the copy wherever it is inserted. Various browsers draw rules differently, but they all appear black and scale to the same width as the browser window. Think of HR as meaning horizontal rule.

Another way to divide documents into sections is by using graphics as rules. You make the graphic rule in a paint program and insert it with the **<IMG>** tag (see page 64). Graphic rules do not change width when the browser screen is resized. The rule does not break the copy unless you use the **<P>** or **
** tags.

You can change the look of the standard non-graphic rule by using optional arguments to the **<HR>** tag. **Size** alters the thickness of a rule measured in pixels. **Width** alters the length measured in pixels or by percent of window width. **Align** shifts the position of rules if they are shorter than the window width. **NoShade** creates a solid, unbeveled rule.

Inserting a dividing rule

<HR>————————**1**

Rules are one way to divide documents into sections.

<HR Size=10 Width=200 Align=Center NoShade>

2   **3**   **4**   **5**

---

1 The <HR> tag inserts a standard rule.

2 Put Size followed by a number of pixels within the <HR> tag to change the thickness of a rule.

3 Put Width followed by the number of pixels or a percent of window width within the <HR> tag to change the length of a rule.

4 Put Align followed by a direction within the <HR> tag to change the position of a rule that is not as wide as the window. Choose between left, right, or center.

5 Put NoShade within the <HR> tag to eliminate the beveled look of rules.

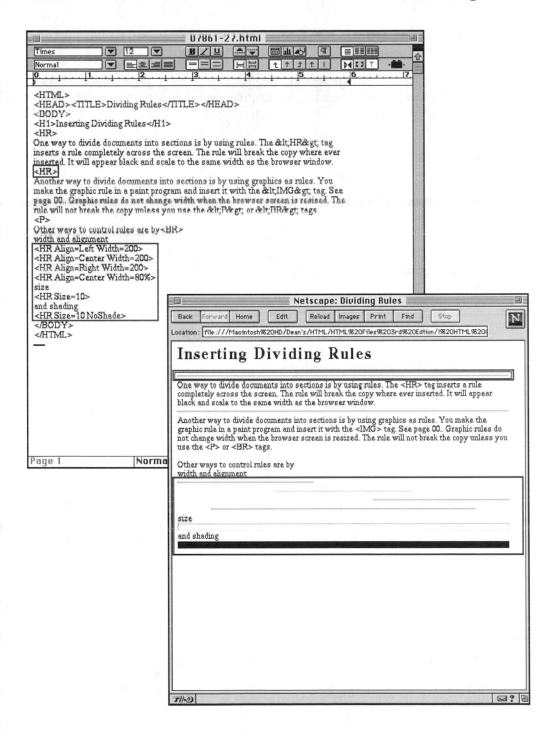

Graphics

Browsers can display graphic images along with text, which makes documents look better. More importantly, images communicate information that would be impossible or too difficult to communicate in words.

You insert a graphic using the **<IMG>** tag and the name of the graphic file. All browsers do not read all file formats. Use the GIF format for saving graphic files; it is read by most graphical browsers.

Remember that graphic files can be big. Big graphics mean even bigger files. Try to keep image files small. Documents with large images or many small ones take a long time to transfer over the Web, usually longer than anyone wants to wait. Often the image is not worth the long load time anyway. Use graphics only when they add information or utility.

One way to speed up load times is by using the **LowSRC** argument with the **<IMG** tag. Create two versions of the graphic, high and low resolution. When the browser loads the HTML file, the low resolution graphic is displayed along with the text. Then the browser retrieves the high resolution graphic replacing the low resolution display.

Type the following example exactly the way it appears to insert a graphic named Clips1.gif and a low resolution file named Clips1BW.gif. To insert your own graphic, just substitute the file names with your own. This works for image files in the same directory as the current Web document. You must specify an URL for a graphic if it is not in the same directory (see page 52).

You should decide on a consistent place to keep graphic files, whether that is in the same directory as the HTML files or not, and a consistent method for refer-ring to graphic files. It is good practice to indicate where the files are with a more specific URL. This guarantees that the graphic files will always be found.

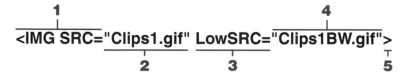

```
<IMG SRC="Clips1.gif" LowSRC="Clips1BW.gif">
```

1 Start with the opening tag <IMG SRC= in front of the file name. Think of SRC as meaning source.

2 Put the graphic file name you want displayed between the quote marks.

3 Include the tag LowSRC= if you want to use a low resolution source.

4 Put the low resolution file name you want displayed between the quote marks.

5 End with a closing tag > after the file name.

Rate	Approximate Transfer Time for 100K File	
2400	8–10 minutes	10–12K per minute
9600	2–4 minutes	40–50K per minute
14400	1.5 minutes	60–80K per minute
28800	0.75 minutes	120–160K per minute

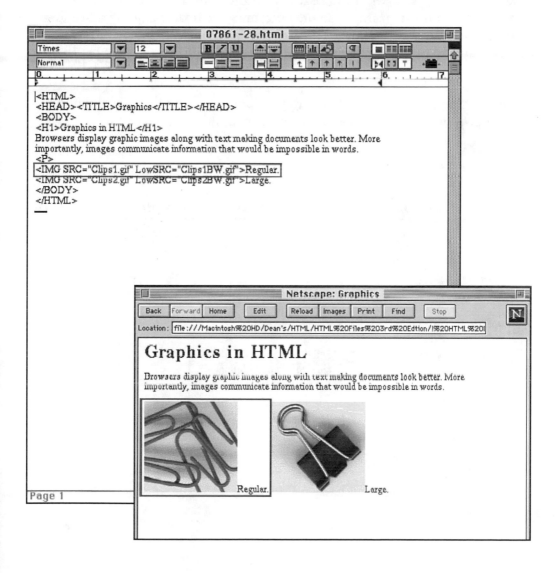

Aligning Graphics

You align graphics with text by using the **ALIGN** attribute within the **<IMG>** tag. There are several alignment options: **top**, **texttop**, **middle**, **absmiddle**, **bottom**, **absbottom**, and **baseline**. Some of these options have the same result when used. Some are subtly different. For example, **bottom** and **baseline** are the same. They both align the baseline of the text with the bottom of the graphic. The **absbottom** option aligns the absolute bottom of the text (including descenders) with the bottom of the graphic. Think of **abs** as meaning absolute.

If you do not specify an alignment, the text aligns with the bottom of the image.

Type the example below exactly the way it appears to insert a graphic named dollar.gif. To insert your own graphic, just substitute the file name with your own.

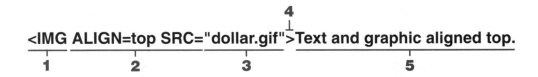

1 Start with the opening <IMG tag.

2 Put the ALIGN= attribute next. Choose the alignment option you want, followed by SRC=.

3 Put the graphic file name you want displayed between the quote marks as the source.

4 End the image tag with a closing > symbol behind the file name.

5 The text can come before or after the image that aligns to it.

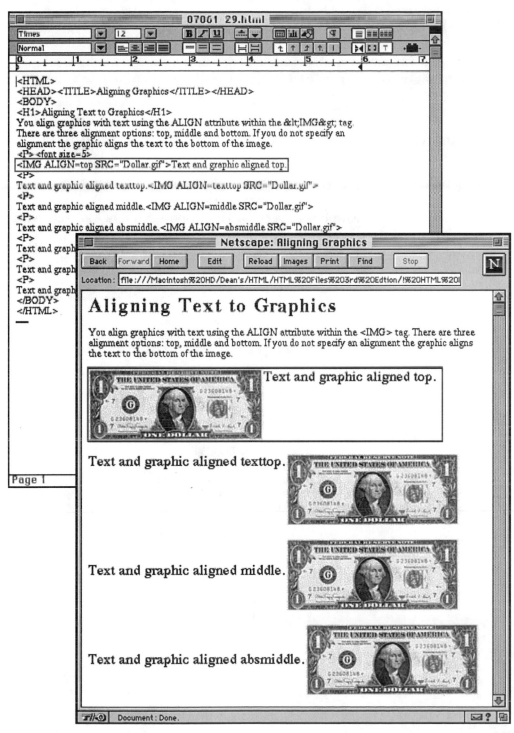

Adding Space Around Graphics

In-line graphics fit snug against other elements on-screen, whether those are above or below or to the right or left. Sometimes this looks funny. So you will want to add extra space.

Add space above and below graphics by including **VSpace** in the **<IMG** tag. Add space to the right and left of graphics by including **HSpace** in the **<IMG** tag. Measure space in pixels.

To nest graphics in text blocks, use either the **Align=left** or **Align=right** arguments to the **<IMG** tag (see page 66). Other alignment options work, but they create odd run-arounds with blocks of copy. These options might look fine with one line of copy or if the graphic is used at the beginning of a paragraph.

To stop text from wrapping around graphics use the **<BR Clear=** tag (see page 36).

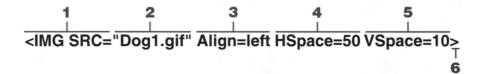

1 Start with the <IMG SRC tag in front of the file name.

2 Put the graphic file name you want displayed between the quote marks.

3 Choose right or left alignment to nest graphics in copy blocks.

4 Put HSpace within the <IMG tag to add space to the right and left of the graphic. Think of the H as meaning horizontal. Put the number of pixels after the = symbol.

5 Put VSpace within the <IMG tag to add space above and below the graphic. Think of the V as meaning vertical. Put the number of pixels after the = symbol.

6 Close the tag with the > symbol.

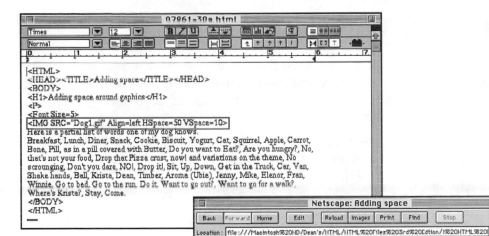

```
|<HTML>
<HEAD><TITLE>Adding space</TITLE></HEAD>
<BODY>
<H1>Adding space around gaphics</H1>
<P>
<Font Size=5>
<IMG SRC="Dog1.gif" Align=left HSpace=50 VSpace=10>
Here is a partial list of words one of my dog knows.
Breakfast, Lunch, Diner, Snack, Cookie, Biscuit, Yogurt, Cat, Squirrel, Apple, Carrot,
Bone, Pill, as in a pill covered with Butter, Do you want to Eat?, Are you hungry?, No,
that's not your food, Drop that Pizza crust, now! and variations on the theme, No
scrounging, Don't you dare, NO!, Drop it!, Sit, Up, Down, Get in the Truck, Car, Van,
Shake hands, Ball, Krista, Dean, Timber, Aroma (Ubie) Jenny, Mike, Elenor, Fran,
Winnie, Go to bed, Go to the run, Do it, Want to go out?, Want to go for a walk?,
Where's Krista?, Stay, Come.
</BODY>
</HTML>
```

Netscape: Adding space

Location: file:///Macintosh%20HD/Dean's/HTML/HTML%20Files%203rd%20Edtion/!%20HTML%20l

Adding space around gaphics

Here is a partial list of words one of my dog knows. Breakfast, Lunch, Diner, Snack, Cookie, Biscuit, Yogurt, Cat, Squirrel, Apple, Carrot, Bone, Pill, as in a pill covered with Butter, Do you want to Eat?, Are you hungry?, No, that's not your food, Drop that Pizza crust, now! and variations on the theme, No scrounging, Don't you dare, NO!, Drop it!, Sit, Up, Down, Get in

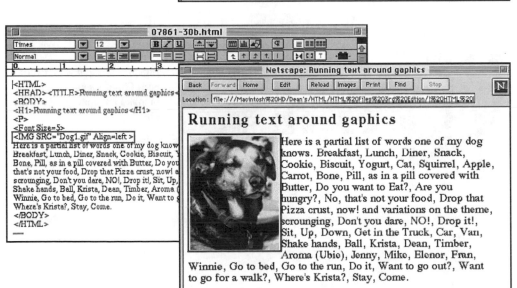

```
|<HTML>
<HEAD><TITLE>Running text around gaphics<
<BODY>
<H1>Running text around gaphics</H1>
<P>
<Font Size=5>
<IMG SRC="Dog1.gif" Align=left >
Here is a partial list of words one of my dog know
Breakfast, Lunch, Diner, Snack, Cookie, Biscuit, Y
Bone, Pill, as in a pill covered with Butter, Do you
that's not your food, Drop that Pizza crust, now! a
scrounging, Don't you dare, NO!, Drop it!, Sit, Up,
Shake hands, Ball, Krista, Dean, Timber, Aroma (
Winnie, Go to bed, Go to the run, Do it, Want to g
Where's Krista?, Stay, Come.
</BODY>
</HTML>
```

Netscape: Running text around gaphics

Location: file:///Macintosh%20HD/Dean's/HTML/HTML%20Files%203rd%20Edtion/!%20HTML%20l

Running text around gaphics

Here is a partial list of words one of my dog knows. Breakfast, Lunch, Diner, Snack, Cookie, Biscuit, Yogurt, Cat, Squirrel, Apple, Carrot, Bone, Pill, as in a pill covered with Butter, Do you want to Eat?, Are you hungry?, No, that's not your food, Drop that Pizza crust, now! and variations on the theme, scrounging, Don't you dare, NO!, Drop it!, Sit, Up, Down, Get in the Truck, Car, Van, Shake hands, Ball, Krista, Dean, Timber, Aroma (Ubie), Jenny, Mike, Elenor, Fran, Winnie, Go to bed, Go to the run, Do it, Want to go out?, Want to go for a walk?, Where's Krista?, Stay, Come.

Transparent Graphics

Most GIF file formats are opaque; even the white parts of the image are not transparent. Opaque and transparent images are always rectangular; you cannot change that. However, silhouetted transparent images seem irregularly shaped and float on the background.

You make opaque GIF files transparent by using converter software. Converters for most platforms are available at FTP archives. (The site at **ftp.ncsa.uiuc.edu** has all the converters listed below.) They all work pretty much the same way. Popular image editors that support transparent GIFs for Windows, Mac, and UNIX are

Platform	Program	Directory and Name at ftp.NCSA.uiuc.edu
Windows	Lview	/Web/Mosaic/Windows/viewers/lviewp1c.zip
Mac	GIF Converter	/Web/Mosaic/Mac/Helpers/gif-converter-237.hqx
UNIX	xv	/Web/Mosaic/Unix/viewers/xv-3.00.tar.Z

Not all images should be transparent. Images with one solid color in the background convert well. Pick appropriate images to avoid odd transparency effects.

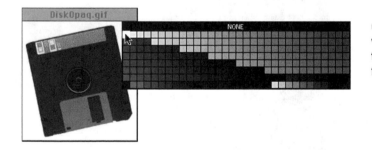

Open the file you want to convert. Choose a color you want to make transparent. Save the file.

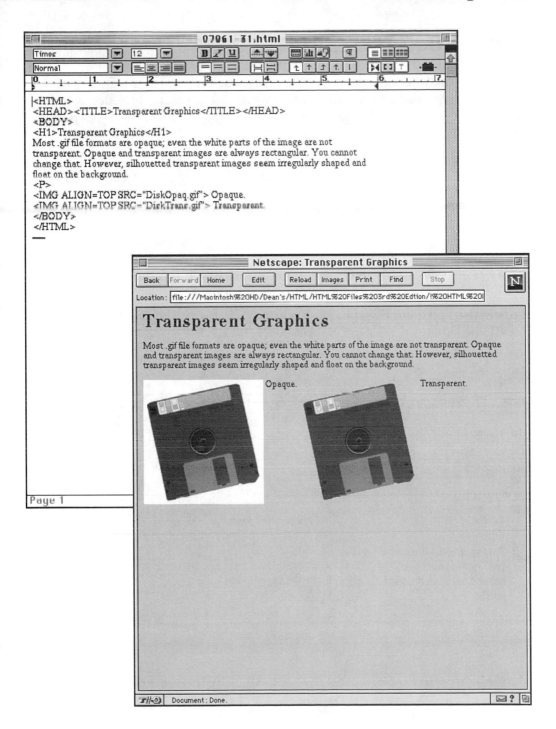

```
<HTML>
<HEAD><TITLE>Transparent Graphics</TITLE></HEAD>
<BODY>
<H1>Transparent Graphics</H1>
Most .gif file formats are opaque; even the white parts of the image are not
transparent. Opaque and transparent images are always rectangular. You cannot
change that. However, silhouetted transparent images seem irregularly shaped and
float on the background.
<P>
<IMG ALIGN=TOP SRC="DiskOpaq.gif"> Opaque.
<IMG ALIGN=TOP SRC="DiskTrans.gif"> Transparent.
</BODY>
</HTML>
```

Backgrounds

Browsers display backgrounds in default colors determined by the preference settings. Backgrounds are usually gray or white. Since color preferences vary from user to user, it is important that you set the background color (see page 44) or create a background graphic.

Background graphics are image files that are repeated like tiles filling the screen no matter how big or small the window. Remember large files mean long load times. Often backgrounds are textures rather than full-color images. Or if they are not textures, they are small simple graphics used to form a wallpaper pattern behind the text.

Be careful about the image you choose for a background. Some images make it hard to read text. Transparent graphics designed for monochromatic backgrounds won't look good on background graphics.

You set the background graphic in the **<Body>** tag at the beginning of an HTML file. If you don't, the background will be a solid color.

1. **Start with the** <BODY **tag.**

2. **Put** Background= **after the opening** <BODY **tag.**

3. **Put the graphic file name you want as the background between the quote marks.**

4. **Put** BGProperties = Fixed **within thr** <BODY> **tag if you do not want the background to scroll with the rest of the screen. Internet Explorer only.**

5. **Close the tag with the** > **symbol.**

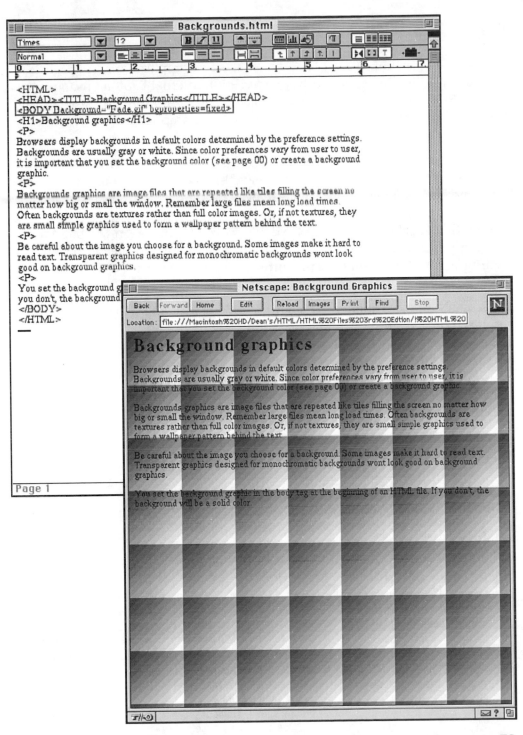

Background Sounds

Browsers can play linked sound files by using helper applications (see page 86) or by using embedded applications (see page 98). Internet Explorer recognizes the **<BGSOUND>** tag, which loads and plays a background sound automatically. The user does not have to click a link to hear it. Netscape can accomplish the same effect by using the **<EMBED>** tag (see page 98).

You place the **<BGSOUND>** or **<EMBED>** tag in the body of the HTML file. The file is sent over the Web along with text and graphics. Remember, sound files can be big. Long clips and higher quality mean even bigger files. Big files take a long time to transfer over the Web and load for playing. That's why it's a good idea to insert either tag at the end of an HTML file. This way the screen will build text and graphics and then load the sound and play it. If you put the tag at the beginning, the screen will be blank until the sound file is retrieved.

The background sound can play once or it can loop for as long as the page is on the screen. Internet Explorer plays both sampled (WAV and AU) and MIDI file formats. For Netscape, LiveAudio plays WAV, AU, AIFF, and MIDI formats. Of course, the user has to have a sound-capable computer system to hear the file play. For Internet Explorer:

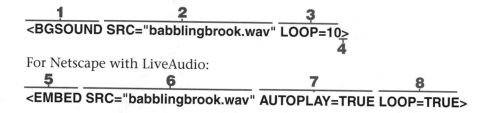

```
          1                    2                  3
<BGSOUND SRC="babblingbrook.wav" LOOP=10>
                                            4
```

For Netscape with LiveAudio:

```
    5                6                    7              8
<EMBED SRC="babblingbrook.wav" AUTOPLAY=TRUE LOOP=TRUE>
```

1 Start with the <BGSOUND tag.

2 Put name of sound file between the quote marks as the source of the background sound. Think of SRC= as meaning source.

3 Put the number of times you want the sound to play after LOOP=.

Choose INFINITE for the sound to repeat indefinitely.

4 Close the tag with the > symbol.

5 Start with the <EMBED tag.

6 Put name of sound file between the quote marks as the source of background sound. Think of SRC= as meaning source.

7 Include the AUTOPLAY= TRUE argument to have the sound start by itself.

8 Include the LOOP=TRUE argument for the sound to repeat indefinitely. Choose FALSE for the sound to play only once.

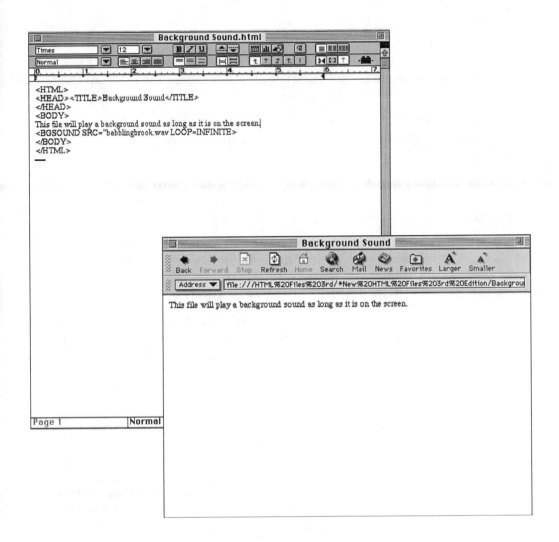

```
<HTML>
<HEAD><TITLE>Background Sound</TITLE>
</HEAD>
<BODY>
This file will play a background sound as long as it is on the screen.
<BGSOUND SRC="babblingbrook.wav LOOP=INFINITE>
</BODY>
</HTML>
```

This file will play a background sound as long as it is on the screen.

Lists

Lists come in two basic varieties: *ordered* (with numbers, letters, or Roman numerals), and *unordered* (with bullets). Both kinds indent the list from the rest of the copy. You can nest lists within each other, as in an outline.

Identify ordered lists with the paired **<OL>** tag and unordered lists with the paired **<UL>** tag. Both lists use the **<LI>** tag for items in the list. The **<LI>** tag is used by itself.

Menu and directory lists also exist as valid HTML tags. However, most browsers do not format these lists differently from ordered, unordered, or glossary lists (see page 76).

You can choose between three types of bullets by including **Type=** within the **<UL>** tag. Specify **disc**, **circle**, or **square**. Sometimes you see Web documents with small graphics in lists instead of bullets. The person who wrote the document inserted small graphics with the **<IMG>** tag (see page 66).

You can choose between numbers, capital letters, lowercase letters, and Roman numerals by including **Type=** within the **<OL>** tag. Specify **1**, **A**, **a,** or **i,** respectively. You can also change the starting point by including **Start=** within the **<OL>** tag. **Type=** also works with the **<LI>** tag.

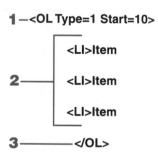

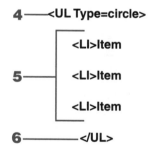

3 Put the </OL> tag after the last item in the list.

4 Start by inserting the <UL> tag in front of the first item in the list. Include the Type of bullet within the <OL> tag.

5 Put the <LI> tag in front of every item in the list. Bullets appear automatically, so you don't need to type them in.

6 Finish by inserting the </UL> tag after the last item in the list.

1 Start by inserting the <OL> tag in front of the first item in the list. Include the Type of numbering system and the Start number within the <OL> tag.

2 Put the <LI> tag in front of every item in the list. Numbers appear automatically, so you don't need to type them in.

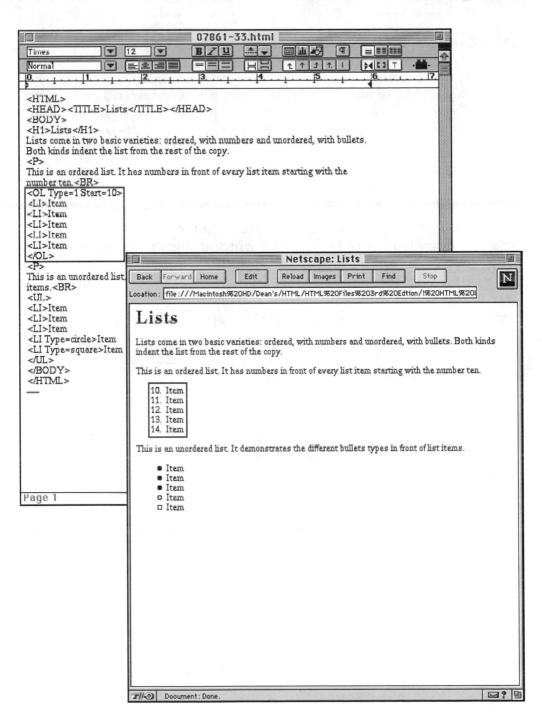

Glossary Lists (Definition Lists)

Glossary lists are meant for lists that have two parts, such as a term and its definition, but they can be used for any similar situation. Glossary lists don't have numbers or bullets, so you need to type them as part of the copy. The **<DL>** tag is used to identify the list, **<DT>** is used for each term, and **<DD>** is used for the definition part. The **<DL>** tag is paired; the **<DT>** and **<DD>** tags are not.

```
<DL>                          1
<DT>Term                      2
<DD>The definition of the term. If the definition is a long
one, the copy will wrap to fit in the window width. The copy
continues to indent as part of the definition. Each term       3
starts on a new line.
<DT>Term
<DD>The definition of the term. If the definition is a long
one, the copy will wrap to fit in the window width. The copy
continues to indent as part of the definition. Each term
starts on a new line.
</DL>                         4
```

1 Start by placing the <DL> tag in front of the first item in the glossary list.

2 Put the <DT> tag in front of every term in the list.

3 Put the <DD> tag in front of every definition in the list.

4 End by putting the </DL> tag after the last item in the glossary list.

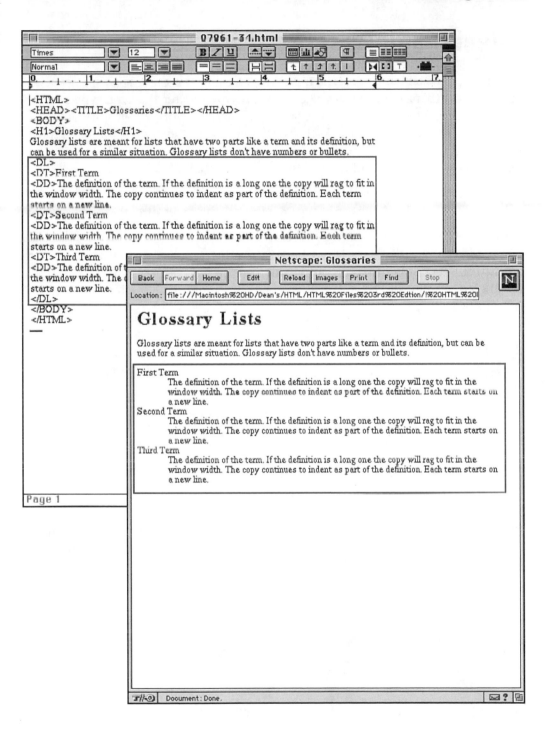

```
<HTML>
<HEAD><TITLE>Glossaries</TITLE></HEAD>
<BODY>
<H1>Glossary Lists</H1>
Glossary lists are meant for lists that have two parts like a term and its definition, but
can be used for a similar situation. Glossary lists don't have numbers or bullets.
<DL>
<DT>First Term
<DD>The definition of the term. If the definition is a long one the copy will rag to fit in
the window width. The copy continues to indent as part of the definition. Each term
starts on a new line.
<DT>Second Term
<DD>The definition of the term. If the definition is a long one the copy will rag to fit in
the window width. The copy continues to indent as part of the definition. Each term
starts on a new line.
<DT>Third Term
<DD>The definition of t
the window width. The
starts on a new line.
</DL>
</BODY>
</HTML>
```

Page 1

Netscape: Glossaries

Back | Forward | Home | Edit | Reload | Images | Print | Find | Stop

Location: file:///Macintosh%20HD/Dean's/HTML/HTML%20Files%203rd%20Edtion/!%20HTML%20I

Glossary Lists

Glossary lists are meant for lists that have two parts like a term and its definition, but can be used for a similar situation. Glossary lists don't have numbers or bullets.

First Term
    The definition of the term. If the definition is a long one the copy will rag to fit in the window width. The copy continues to indent as part of the definition. Each term starts on a new line.
Second Term
    The definition of the term. If the definition is a long one the copy will rag to fit in the window width. The copy continues to indent as part of the definition. Each term starts on a new line.
Third Term
    The definition of the term. If the definition is a long one the copy will rag to fit in the window width. The copy continues to indent as part of the definition. Each term starts on a new line.

Document: Done.

Special and Reserved Characters

The only characters you can type in HTML documents are the letters, numbers, and symbols that appear on your keyboard. Any character that you type by holding down a key other than the Shift key may not work when someone views your document over the Web. That's because not every computer uses the same combination of keys to mean the same special character. Bullets, accented letters, ©, ™, ®, å, π, £, and ¢ fall into the special character set.

The HTML language reserves some characters for code only, for example, the ", &, <, and > symbols. You cannot type a reserved character directly in the text of your document.

Use named or numbered entities whenever you need a special or reserved character in the text of your document. Named entities use abbreviations, while numbered entities use the ASCII numbers to indicate the character (see page 193 for an ASCII list).

Named Entities

1 —— < —— 3

2

1 Start with an & in front of the abbreviation.

2 Put the abbreviation next.

3 End with a ; (semicolon) after the abbreviation.

Numbered Entities

4

£ — 6

5

4 Start with an &# in front of the ASCII number.

5 Put the ASCII number next.

6 End with a ; after the ASCII number.

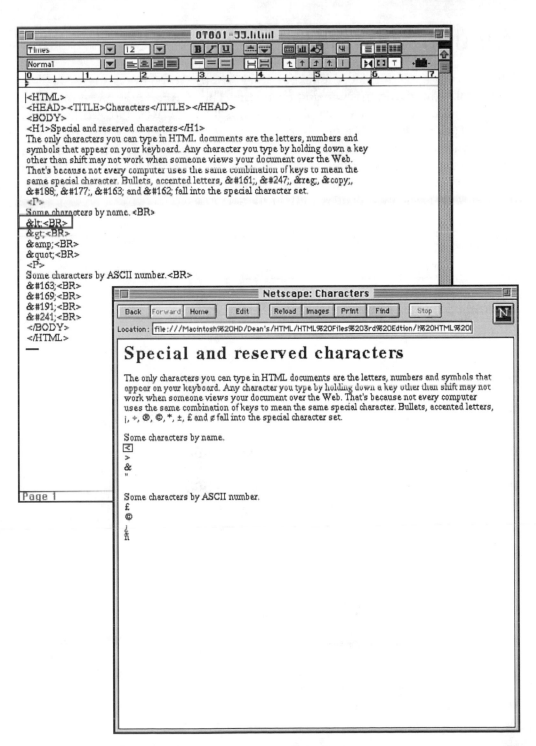

Preformatted Type

A browser normally formats the text in an HTML file and ignores any extra spaces, tabs, or line returns you add to the file. The **<PRE>** tag, however, formats the text based on the way you type it. It retains all the spaces, tabs, and returns in the HTML file so that it looks exactly the same when viewed with a browser. There's one catch: the text appears in monospaced type, like Courier. Charts that don't use the **<TABLE>** tag (see page 118) are usually created with the **<PRE>** tag. Always use a monospaced font when creating preformatted text so that the spacing reflects the final display in the browser.

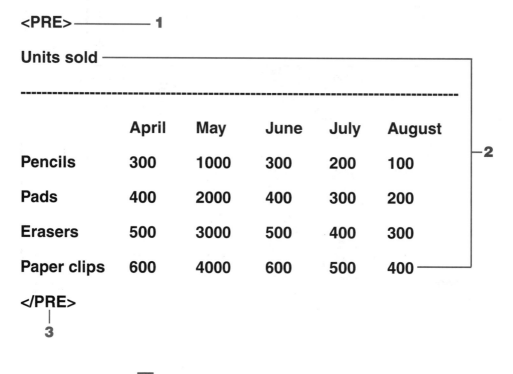

<PRE> —————— 1

Units sold —————————————————————————

	April	May	June	July	August
Pencils	300	1000	300	200	100
Pads	400	2000	400	300	200
Erasers	500	3000	500	400	300
Paper clips	600	4000	600	500	400

—2

</PRE>

3

1 Start by putting the <PRE> tag in front of the text.

2 Put the text you want to style between the tags.

3 Put the </PRE> tag after the text.

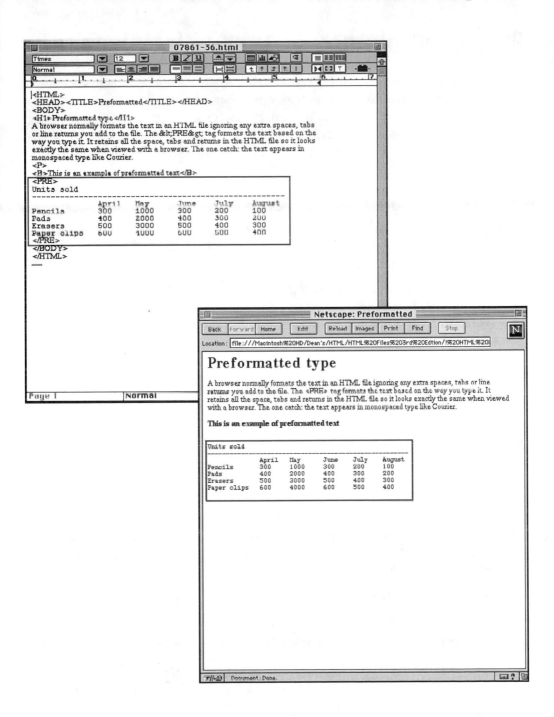

Multiple Columns of Text with Netscape

Normally, text on the screen runs in lines that are as wide as the browser window. This means that unless either the copy wraps around graphics or line breaks are inserted to shorten the line length, blocks of copy can be very wide. In fact, they can be as wide as the user's screen. Most people find long lines hard to read. That is why newspapers, magazines, and some books are set with two or more columns of text on a page.

The **<MULTICOL>** tag creates columns of text without resorting to setting up a table. Copy flows from one column to the next, from top to bottom, left to right, filling the columns evenly across the screen. To create multiple columns, surround text with the opening and closing **<MULTICOL>** tags. It is just like any other paired text formatting tag.

There are three arguments to the **<MULTICOL>** tag. **COLS=** defines the number of columns. **GUTTER=** defines the size of the space between the columns. **WIDTH=** defines the total width of the columns and gutters combined. Measure gutter and width in pixels.

```
        1        2         3         4     5
<MULTICOL  COLS=3 GUTTER=10 WIDTH=288>
```

This is copy that is broken into three columns.
                            6

```
</MULTICOL>
     7
```

1 Start with the <MULTICOL tag to break copy into more than one column.

2 Include COL=, followed by a number, within the <MULTICOL tag to set the number of columns.

3 Include GUTTER=, followed by a number, within the <MULTICOL tag to set the size of the space between columns.

4 Include WIDTH=, followed a number, within the <MULTICOL tag to set the width of the columns and gutters combined.

5 Close the table with the <MULTICOL tag with the > symbol.

6 Put the text you want to appear in columns between the opening and closing <MULTICOL> tags.

7 Close the table with the </MULTICOL> tag.

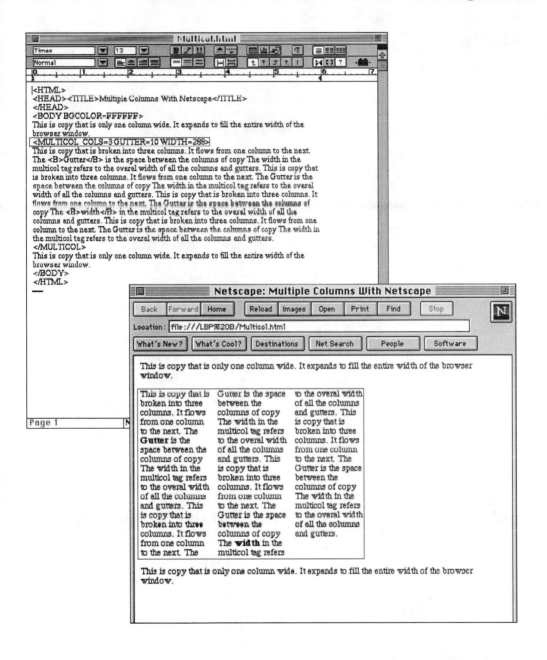

Sound and Video with Helper Applications

It is possible to include sound and video in your HTML documents. You insert sound and video files as you do linked text or graphics.

Although many browsers are adding sound and video extensions, most browsers do not play sound or video, they only retrieve the file. Another program takes over from there, and that's one of the problems. You don't know if the people trying to see or hear your file have the right software and hardware. If they do, it is still hard to choose a file format available for all platforms. The best you can do is tell them the file format you picked and let them determine whether or not they can use it.

There are very few cross-platform file formats. For sound, AIFF for the Macintosh and WAV for Windows are common formats. For video, the MPEG format is common and viewers are available for Windows, Mac, and UNIX. QuickTime is also a common format that can be viewed in Windows and Macs. You may opt for other formats, just remember to mention whichever you choose in the text.

Remember sound and video files are big. Long clips and higher quality mean even bigger files. Big files take a long time to transfer over the Web. That's why it's a good idea to put the file size in the text so people know how long the file takes to load.

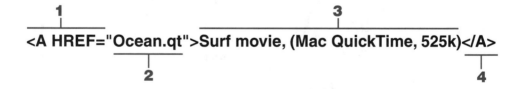

1

3

`<A HREF="Ocean.qt">Surf movie, (Mac QuickTime, 525k)</A>`

2

4

1 Start with the opening tag `<A HREF=` in front of the file name.

2 Put the file name of the sound or video between the quote marks.

3 Put the text you want people to click between the `>` and `<` symbols. Include the file size and format.

4 End with a closing tag `</A>` after the text.

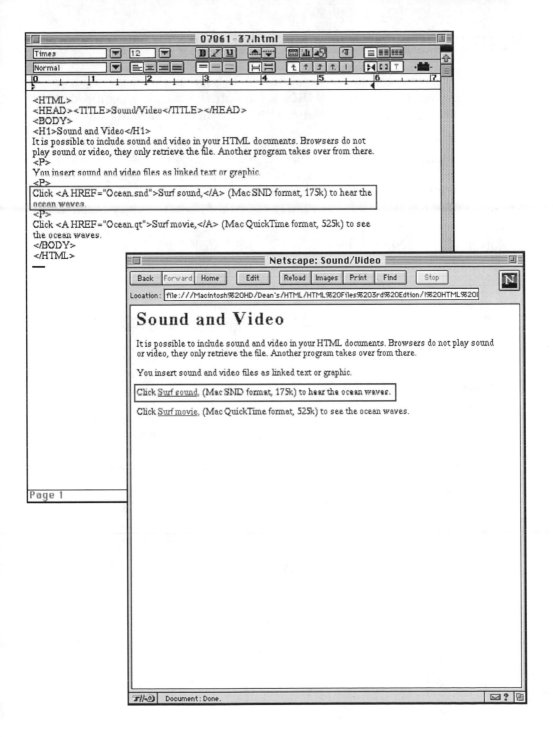

Using Video with Internet Explorer

Internet Explorer has an extension to the **<IMG>** tag that allows you to insert video files in Web pages. The **DYNSRC=** argument works with an embedded video application or, more commonly, with a system extension like QuickTime.

The **DYNSRC=** extension is very new and some of the arguments to it are buggy. Below is a description of the basics; how to insert, start, and loop the video. Other arguments include **LOOPDELAY=**, which pauses between each playback, and **CONTROLS**, which adds a control panel to the video image. **VOLUME=** is sure to be added in the future. You can define the size of the video image by using the **WIDTH=** and **HEIGHT=** arguments to the **<IMG>** tag. However, picture resolution is predetermined by the original file. Usually, quality suffers when changing size.

1 Start with the <IMG tag to insert a graphic; see page 64.

2 Include DYNSRC= and the name of the video file within the <IMG tag. Put the file name in quotes. Think of DYNSRC as meaning dynamic source.

3 Include START= to define when you want the video to begin playing. Choose OPENFILE to start automatically or MOUSEOVER to start when the user points to the graphic.

4 Include LOOP=, followed by a number, within the <IMG tag to define how many times the video replays. Choose any number or use INFINITE to have the video play repeatedly until a new page is loaded.

5 Close the <IMG tag with the > symbol.

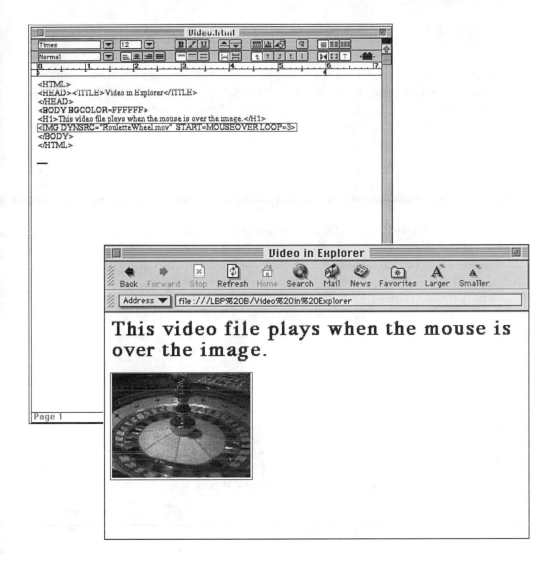

Image Maps—Using CGI Scripts

Normally, clicking any spot on a linked graphic is the same as clicking any other spot. One link per graphic is the rule. But with server-side *image maps,* a graphic contains more than one link. Clicking different spots takes you to different files. To function properly, image maps require several files and a gateway script to run on the server.

First, choose the graphic for the image map. Not every graphic is appropriate for mapping. Choose graphics that have clearly defined sections or labels. Prompts in the text help clarify that the image on the screen contains multiple links.

Next, create a file containing the coordinates of the different sections of the graphic. If the shape is circular, specify the center of the circle and the radius. If the shape is rectangular, specify the upper-left and lower-right corners of the rectangle. If the shape is a polygon, specify all corner points. If the shape is a single point, specify the point. The upper-left corner of a graphic is 0,0. The format of the coordinates is different, depending on the type of server used. If shapes overlap, their order in the coordinate file determines which lies on top.

Last, you need a gateway script available on the server that takes the mouse click coordinates from the browser, looks them up in the coordinate file, and opens the correct link.

The link

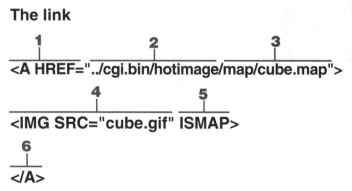

The Coordinate File Following the CERN Standards

1	Start by creating a link.
2	Put the URL of the gateway script you need here.
3	Put the complete URL of the file containing the map coordinates here.
4	Insert a graphic.
5	Include the argument ISMAP so that the browser knows to send the mouse click coordinates to the gateway script.
6	End with the link's closing tag.

polygon (193, 46) (193, 144) (146, 93) (46, 93) http://myDomain/myfolder/top.html

7 Start with the type of shape.

rectangle (46,193) (146, 93) (146, 193) (46, 193) http: // myDomain/myfolder/top.html

8 Put each coordinate needed to describe the shape between parentheses.

The Coordinate File Following the NCSA Standards

9 End with the complete URL of the linked file.

10   **11**

polygon http://myDomain/myfolder/top.html
150,46 193,46 146,93 46,93

10 Start with the type of shape.

12

polygon http://myDomain/myfolder/top.html
(193, 46) (193, 46) (146, 93) (146, 93)

11 Put the complete URL of the linked file next.

rectangle http://myDomain/myfolder/top.html
(46, 93) (146, 93) (146, 193) (46, 193)

12 End with each coordinate needed to describe the shape. Do not use parentheses.

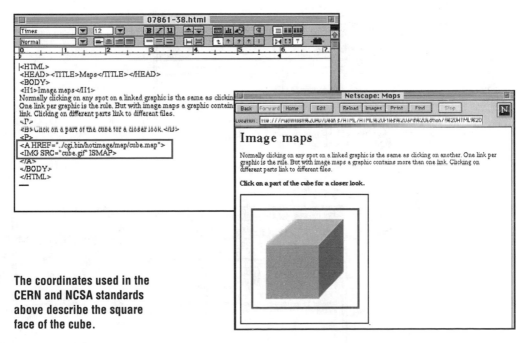

The coordinates used in the CERN and NCSA standards above describe the square face of the cube.

Image Maps—Using Browsers

User-side image maps are similar to server-side image maps (see page 90) in that they contain more than one link per graphic. Clicking different parts takes you to different files. Image maps require several files and a gateway script to run on the server; however, user-side image maps do not because they work on the user side. The mouse click coordinates are interpreted by the browser and not by the server. This saves transfer time and eliminates the need for gateway scripts that interpret image map coordinates. Remember, not all browsers support use maps.

First, choose the graphic for the user-side image map. Not every graphic is appropriate for mapping. Choose graphics that have clearly defined sections or labels. Prompts in the text will help people understand that the image on their screen contains multiple links.

Next, create a **<MAP>** tag within the same HTML file that contains the coordinates of the different sections and the links. If the shape is circular, specify the center of the circle and the radius. If the shape is rectangular, specify the upper-left and lower-right corners of the rectangle. If the shape is a polygon, specify all corner points. If the shape is a single point, specify the point. The upper-left corner of a graphic is 0,0. If shapes overlap, their order in the coordinate file determines which lies on top.

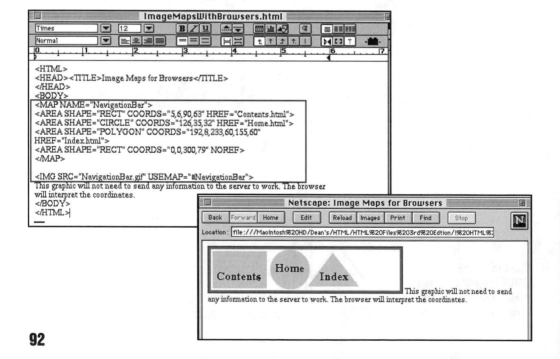

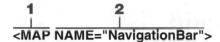

1   **2**

`<MAP NAME="NavigationBar">`

3   **4**   **5**   **6**

`<AREA SHAPE="RECT" COORDS="5,6,90,63" HREF="Contents.html">`

`<AREA SHAPE="CIRCLE" COORDS="126,35,32" HREF="Home.html">`

`<AREA SHAPE="POLYGON" COORDS="192,8,233,60,155,60" HREF="Index.html">`

                        7   **8**

`<AREA SHAPE="RECT" COORDS="0,0,300,79" NOHREF> </MAP>`

        9   **10**   **11**   **12**

`<IMG SRC="NavigationBar.gif" USEMAP="#NavigationBar">`

1 Start with the opening `<MAP` tag.

2 Put the name of the use map within the quote marks.

3 Start each section of the use map you define with the `<AREA` tag.

4 Put the shape of the area within the quotes that follow the SHAPE= argument. Choose RECT, CIRCLE, POLYGON, or POINT.

5 Put the coordinates of the shape within the quotes that follow the COORDS= argument.

6 Put the URL of the link within the quotes that follow the HREF= argument.

7 If the shape has no link put NOHREF instead of HREF and the URL of the link.

8 Close the definition of the use map shapes with the `</MAP>` tag.

9 Insert the graphic using the `<IMG>` tag (see page 64).

10 Include the argument USEMAP so that the browser knows to use the mouse click coordinates with the map tag coordinates.

11 Put the name of the map preceded by a # symbol within the quotes that follow the USEMAP= argument.

12 Close the `<IMG` tag with a `>` symbol.

Scripts Within HTML Documents

Scripts are programs that are typed as part of HTML documents. They add function to Web pages that is not possible with standard HTML tags. Scripts are similar to external applications but must be written in a language that the browser can understand. This means JavaScript for Netscape, VBScript and JScript for Internet Explorer. Both of these are based on, or subsets of, larger programming languages; Java and Visual Basic. The scripting languages are limited so programs cannot be created that do harm to the user's computer.

Place a script within the **<HEAD>** of the HTML file. A script loads as the file is read by the browser. The script runs when an event placed somewhere else in the file is triggered. In the following example, the event **onLoad** is put within the **<BODY>** tag so that the script starts immediately. Events also can be clicks or rollovers.

To learn more about writing your own scripts in JavaScript or VBScript, visit Netscape's or MicroSoft's Web sites. Many scripts are made public on the Web. Use a search engine to locate them.

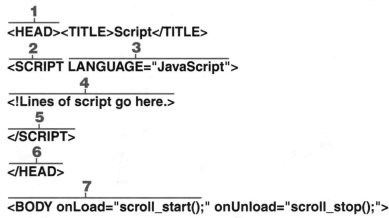

1
`<HEAD><TITLE>Script</TITLE>`

2   **3**
`<SCRIPT LANGUAGE="JavaScript">`

4
`<!Lines of script go here.>`

5
`</SCRIPT>`

6
`</HEAD>`

7
`<BODY onLoad="scroll_start();" onUnload="scroll_stop();">`

1 Start with the <HEAD> tag.

2 Put the <SCRIPT tag within the <HEAD> of the file.

3 Put the name of the scripting language between the quote marks. Choose JavaScript for Netscape and VBScript for Internet Explorer.

4 Put the entire script between the comment tags. This way, browsers that don't recognize the script tag will ignore the script.

5 End the script with the closing </SCRIPT> tag.

6 End the head with the closing </HEAD> tag.

7 Put an event somewhere in the file to trigger the script.

94

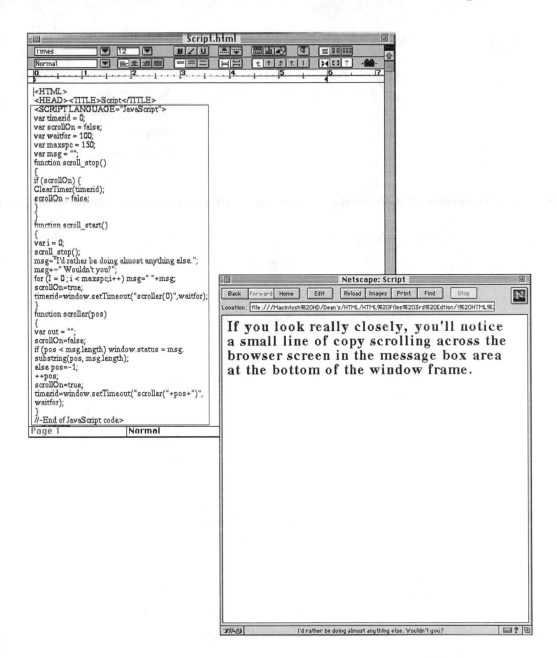

```
<HTML>
<HEAD><TITLE>Script</TITLE>
<SCRIPT LANGUAGE="JavaScript">
var timerid = 0;
var scrollOn = false;
var waitfor = 100;
var maxspc = 150;
var msg = "";
function scroll_stop()
{
if (scrollOn) {
ClearTimer(timerid);
scrollOn = false;
}
}
function scroll_start()
{
var i = 0;
scroll_stop();
msg="I'd rather be doing almost anything else.";
msg+=" Wouldn't you?";
for (I = 0; i < maxspc;i++) msg=" "+msg;
scrollOn=true;
timerid=window.setTimeout("scroller(0)",waitfor);
}
function scroller(pos)
{
var out = "";
scrollOn=false;
if (pos < msg.length) window.status = msg.
substring(pos, msg.length);
else pos=-1;
++pos;
scrollOn=true;
timerid=window.setTimeout("scroller("+pos+")",
waitfor);
}
//-End of JavaScript code>
```

Page 1   Normal

Netscape: Script

Location: file:///Macintosh%20HD/Dean's/HTML/HTML%20Files%203rd%20Edtion/!%20HTML%:

If you look really closely, you'll notice a small line of copy scrolling across the browser screen in the message box area at the bottom of the window frame.

I'd rather be doing almost anything else. Wouldn't you?

Java Applets—Using External Applications

External applications are mini-programs, called applets, that are written in the Java programming language. They add function to Web pages that is not possible with helper applications, plug-ins, or CGI scripts. If you have a Java-enhanced browser, chances are you have seen a Java applet. They can be games, stock tickers, animations, or calculators. You name it—Applets are limited only by a programmer's talent and the safeguards built into the Java interpreter. Safeguards prevent talented but evil programmers from creating applets that can do damage to a user's computer.

Although applets are written in Java, they are not typed into the HTML file using the **<SCRIPT>** tag (see page 94). Instead, applets sit on the server with the rest of the files that may be necessary for a Web page (for example, graphics, sound, video). The browser retrieves the source code just like a graphics file. The Java-enhanced browser then interprets the code and displays the applet on the screen.

Use the **<APPLET>** tag to insert an applet in your HTML file. The only arguments needed within the tag are **CODE=**, which identifies the source file, and **WIDTH=** and **HEIGHT=**, which create a rectangular space for the applet. **<PARAM>** is an associated tag that passes information to the applet. You control aspects of the applet with **NAME= VALUE=** pairs included within the **<PARAM>** tag. Not all applets need parameters—check the documentation of the applet you are using.

Writing an applet goes beyond the scope of this book. For more on the subject, try *Special Edition Using Java* (Que, 1996). Many applets are also available publicly. Search the Web for applet archives and documentation.

```
     1              2                    3
<APPLET CODE="AllLights.class" WIDTH=280 HEIGHT=200>
                                                   4

<PARAM NAME=COLOR VALUE="YELLOW">

<PARAM NAME=LOOSERTEXT VALUE="Try again later.">
5
<PARAM NAME=WINNERTEXT VALUE="Nice going.">
     6
</APPLET>
```

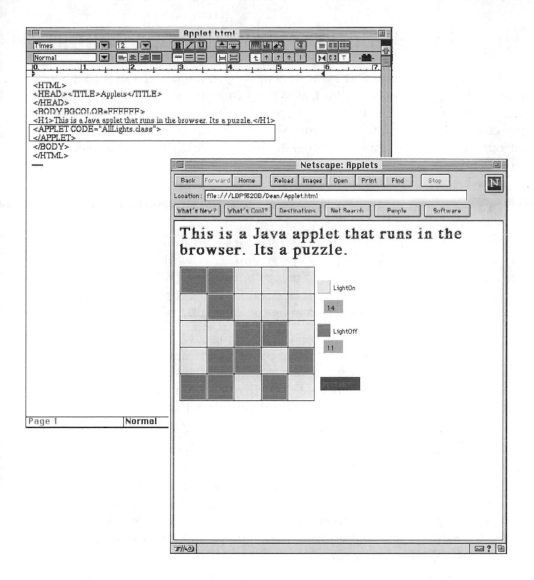

1 Start with the <APPLET tag to insert an external application.

2 Include CODE= and the name of the file within the <APPLET tag. Put the file name in quotes.

3 Create a space in which the applet appears by including the WIDTH= and HEIGHT= arguments, followed a number. Measure in pixels.

4 Close the opening <APPLET tag with the > symbol.

5 If the applet requires parameters to work, include the <PARAM> tags between the opening and closing <APPLET> tags.

6 Close with the </APPLET> tag.

Plug-Ins—Using Embedded Applications

HTML and the Web started as a way of accessing text and graphics through a point and click interface. However, as Web surfing grows and large corporate sites go online, there is a drive to go beyond the basics. Today, Web pages are expected to deliver sound, video, and custom applications. JavaScript and VBScript add power to browsers. Programmers can write their own applets and novices can use publicly available applets (see page 96). Another way to keep up with the Websters is to use helper applications, or plug-ins.

Helper applications are standard software that a user might have for other purposes. Plug-ins are more like system extensions. Instead of launching a separate application and opening a file from within that application, plug-ins are, in a way, already loaded when the browser starts up. They work like plug-ins for other software (for example, QuarkXpress, Photoshop). The browser looks to see which plug-ins are available when it launches and then uses these plug-ins for added functionality when called upon by the **<EMBED>** tag.

Netscape and Internet Explorer have different plug-ins for the same functions. So, you have to deal with cross-platform issues. Even control arguments can differ for two similar plugs-ins on the same platform. One strategy is to tell users which browser to use for optimal viewing of your site. Another strategy is to write code for the plug-ins that ship with the browser you prefer.

The **<EMBED>** tag is how you use these plug-ins. For example, you can insert a sound in Netscape by using the LiveAudio plug-in. The tag identifies the sound file. The browser automatically uses LiveAudio to play the sound. LiveAudio gives you HTML arguments to display a control panel, preset the volume, determine when the sound starts playing, and how many times it repeats. With these controls, it is possible to create a background sound in Netscape without using the **<BGSOUND>** tag, which only Internet Explorer supports (see page 74). Just set the **AUTOSTART=** and **LOOP=** arguments to **TRUE**.

The **<NOEMBED>** tag displays alternate text if the browser does not support plug-ins. Usually, a text link downloads a file to the user's computer for use with a helper application.

```
    1              2
<EMBED SRC="HornFanfare.aiff"
                      3
CONTROLS=CONSOLE VOLUME=50 AUTOSTART=TRUE LOOP=TRUE
```

_____4_____5_

WIDTH=144 HEIGHT=60>

<NOEMBED>

<A SRC="HornFanfare.aiff">

Play the music with a helper application.</A>

—6

4 Control the size of the plug-in when a control panel is displayed with the WIDTH= and HEIGHT= arguments. Measure in pixels.

1 Start with the <EMBED tag to use a plug-in.

2 Include SRC= and the name of the file that uses the plug-in within the <EMBED tag. Put the file name in quotes.

3 Include within the <EMBED tag any other plug-in arguments needed to set variables. Check documentation for each plug-in.

5 Close the <EMBED tag with the > symbol.

6 Put a link (in this case explanatory text) between the <NOEMBED> and </NOEMBED> tags for browsers that do not support plug-ins.

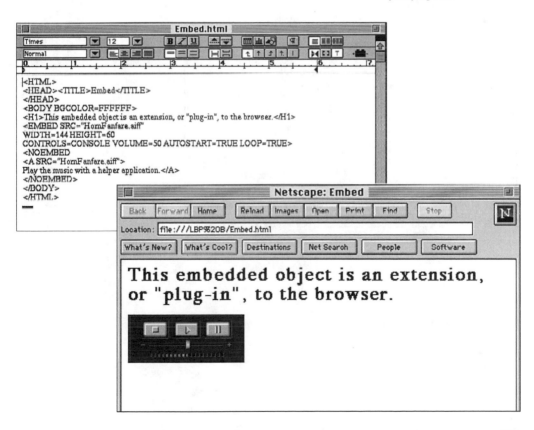

What Is a Form?

A *form* is a special part of the body of an HTML document. It allows users to input text and make choices from check boxes, radio buttons, and selection lists. You design forms for your specific purposes by combining these input types.

Forms are often literally just that, forms for gathering information. Purchase orders, registration cards, applications, and exams all fall into this category. The browser sends the user input to an e-mail address.

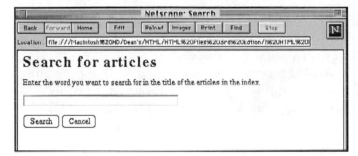

Forms are used for defining search parameters. The browser sends the input to the server for processing. The result returns for display on your screen.

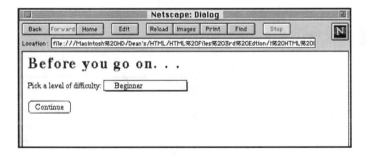

Forms are used for dialog boxes. A choice defines which branch of a document you enter.

How Forms Work

A form works in conjunction with a gateway script on a server to process the information submitted to it. Writing scripts requires a higher level of programming expertise than what is covered in this book. A good source for getting started with gateway scripts is Que's *Special Edition Using HTML 3.2, Third Edition* by Tom Savola.

If you don't know any programming languages except HTML, you will find it easier to ask for help from the staff at your server. Ask the staff if they have a script you can use.

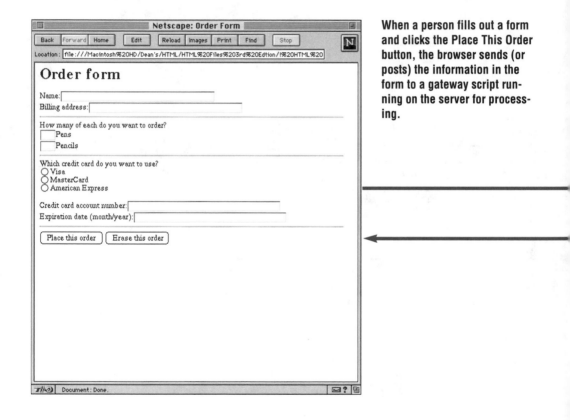

When a person fills out a form and clicks the Place This Order button, the browser sends (or posts) the information in the form to a gateway script running on the server for processing.

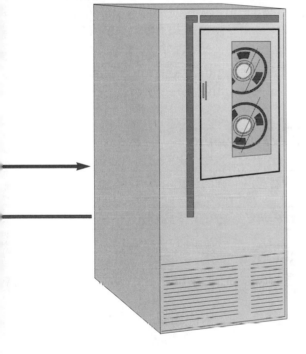

Information passed from the browser to the server is processed by a gateway script. The processed information is sent back to the browser or forwarded to another location.

Basic Form Programming Elements

You must place a form inside the body of an HTML document. That means that every form has all the same tags required at the top and bottom of any other HTML document (see page 20).

Forms consist of three basic parts: the opening tag, the input types, and the submit button. The opening tag, **<FORM>**, defines the method by which the information gets to the gateway script and the name of the script itself. Input types, using the tag **<input type>**, include text fields, check boxes, radio buttons, and selection lists (see pages 106,110-114). A special input type, **hidden**, allows you to include additional information in the form to the gateway script. The submit button, **<input type=submit value="Submit">**, is used to send the choices in the form to the gateway script. An image map also can function as a graphic send button and link (see page 116). Additionally, a cancel button, **<input type=reset value="Clear">**, is used to clear or reset default choices in the form.

You can put more than one form in an HTML document and any number of input types within a single form. However, you cannot nest forms.

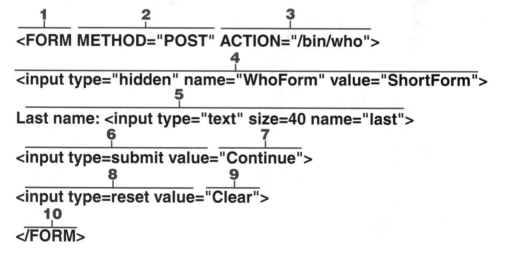

```
                1              2                      3
<FORM METHOD="POST" ACTION="/bin/who">
                                     4
<input type="hidden" name="WhoForm" value="ShortForm">
                     5
Last name: <input type="text" size=40 name="last">
              6                    7
<input type=submit value="Continue">
              8                    9
<input type=reset value="Clear">
        10
</FORM>
```

1 Start the form with the <FORM> tag.

2 Use POST for the method of submitting the information to the gateway script.

3 Put the URL of the gateway script that you want to process the information between the quote marks as the action.

4 Put the input type hidden if you want to send additional information to the CGI script that the user does not see.

5 Put all other text and input types after the opening tag.

6 Put a submit button in your form to send the information to the gateway scripts.

7 Put the copy you want to appear in the submit button between the quote marks.

8 Put a reset button in your form to clear the form.

9 Put the copy that you want to appear in the reset button between the quote marks.

10 End every form with </FORM>.

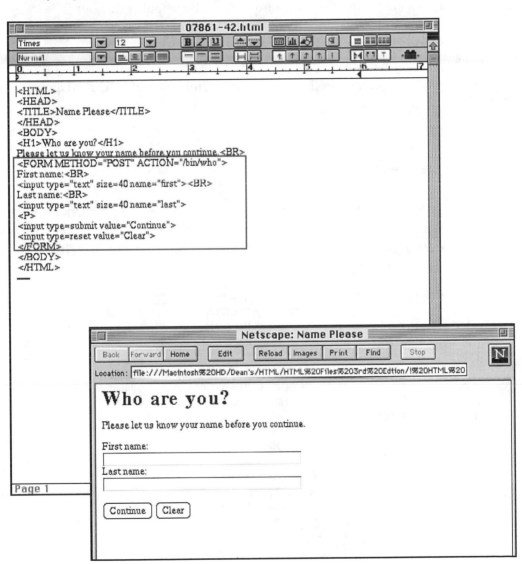

Text Fields

Text fields in forms enable a person to enter a word, phrase, or series of numbers. Text appears in the field when entered by the user. If you specify password as the input type instead of text, bullets hide anything entered from view.

You must include a size and name for each text field. Optional parameters include setting a maximum length for input and the default value of the field. The default value shows up in the field when the form first loads or when the reset button is pressed.

The browser sends the information in the field when the user clicks the submit button in the form. It attaches the name to the information in the field as an identifier.

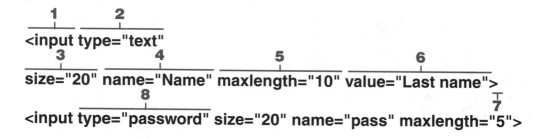

1 Start with the <input tag.

2 Put text between the quote marks as the type of input.

3 Put the length of the text field you want between the quote marks as the size.

4 Put a label you want attached to this information between the quote marks as the name of input.

5 Put the maximum number of characters allowed in the field between the quote marks as the maxlength.

6 Put the copy you want to use as the default for the field between the quote marks as the value.

7 End with a closing > symbol.

8 Use password between the quote marks as the type if you want the input to appear as bullets on the screen.

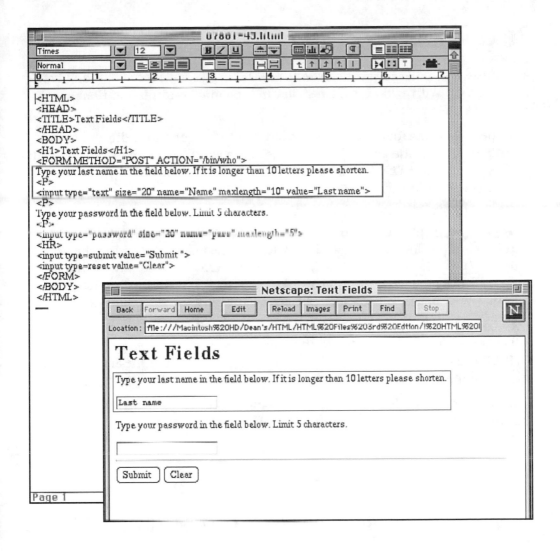

Text Areas

Text areas are similar to text fields in forms. Text areas have scroll bars and text fields do not. With a text area, a person can type more information than usually fits in a text field.

You specify a name for each text area as well as its height and width dimensions. **ROWS** defines the height and **COLS** defines the width. You can include default text as part of the **<TEXTAREA** tag. It will appear in the text area when the page first appears on-screen.

You can also control how text wraps as it is typed in a text area by including the **WRAP=** argument within the **<TEXTAREA** tag. When wrapping is off, text continues as one long line beyond the width of the text area, causing the user either to break the lines with the Enter key or to scroll horizontally to read the text. By setting the wrap to either **WRAP=Virtual** or **WRAP=Physical**, text automatically breaks at the width of the text area, just as you would expect it to.

By setting the wrap to **WRAP=Virtual**, no line breaks are sent to the server when the Submit button in the form is clicked. By setting the wrap to **WRAP=Physical**, all line breaks are sent to the server when the Submit button in the form is clicked. This can be important when processing the information.

The browser sends information in the text area to the server when the Submit button in the form is clicked. It attaches the name to the information in the field as an identifier.

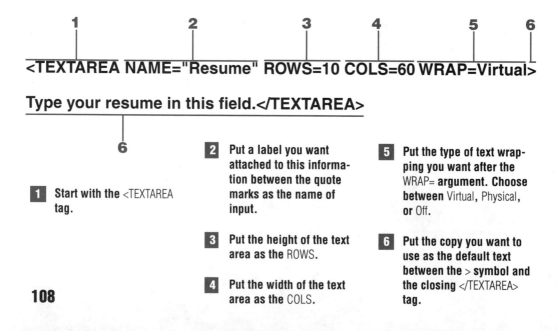

```
<TEXTAREA NAME="Resume" ROWS=10 COLS=60 WRAP=Virtual>
Type your resume in this field.</TEXTAREA>
```

1 Start with the `<TEXTAREA` tag.

2 Put a label you want attached to this information between the quote marks as the name of input.

3 Put the height of the text area as the ROWS.

4 Put the width of the text area as the COLS.

5 Put the type of text wrapping you want after the WRAP= argument. Choose between Virtual, Physical, or Off.

6 Put the copy you want to use as the default text between the > symbol and the closing </TEXTAREA> tag.

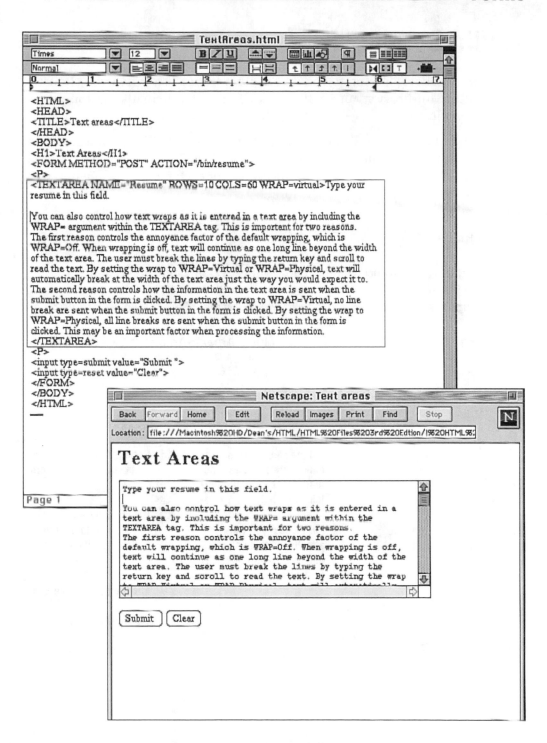

Radio Buttons

Radio buttons allow a person to choose one item from a list. When you choose a radio button, the browser automatically deselects any other radio button you previously selected.

You must include a name and value for each radio button. The default selection shows up in the field when the form first loads or when the user clicks the reset button. The browser sends the name and value for each radio button when the user clicks the submit button in the form.

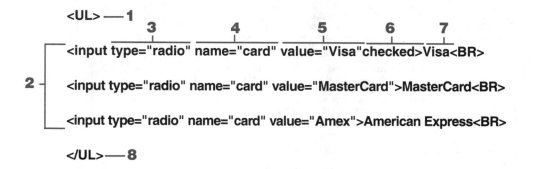

1 Start by creating a list.	**4** Put the same text for the name between the quote marks for each radio button in the list.	**6** Set the default as selected by including the word checked.
2 Put the input tag in front of each radio button.		
3 Type radio between the quote marks as the type of input.	**5** Put the text you want attached to this selection between the quote marks as the value.	**7** Put the copy you want to appear next to the radio button after the closing > symbol.
		8 End the list with the </UL> tag.

Check Boxes

Check boxes allow a person to choose one or more items from a list. When you choose a check box, the browser leaves selected any other check boxes you previously selected.

You must include a name and value for each check box. The default selection(s) shows up in the field when the form first loads or when the user clicks the reset button. The browser sends the name and value for each check box when the user clicks the submit button in the form.

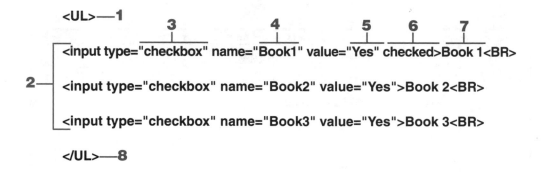

```
<UL>—1
                    3                    4              5     6      7
<input type="checkbox" name="Book1" value="Yes" checked>Book 1<BR>

2— <input type="checkbox" name="Book2" value="Yes">Book 2<BR>

   <input type="checkbox" name="Book3" value="Yes">Book 3<BR>

   </UL>—8
```

1 Start by creating a list.

2 Put the <input tag in front of each check box.

3 Put checkbox between the quote marks as the type of input.

4 Put the different text for the name between the quote marks for each check box in the list.

5 Put the same text for the value between the quote marks for each check box in the list.

6 Set the default for each check box you want selected by including the word checked.

7 Put the copy you want to appear next to the check box after the closing > symbol.

8 End the listwith the </UL> tag.

```
<HTML>
<HEAD>
<TITLE>Check boxes</TITLE>
</HEAD>
<BODY>
<H1>Making a few choices</H1>
<FORM METHOD="POST" ACTION="/bin/card">
Which book do you want to order? <BR>
<UL>
<input type="checkbox" name="Book1" value="Yes" checked>Book 1<BR>
<input type="checkbox" name="Book2" value="Yes">Book 2<BR>
<input type="checkbox" name="Book3" value="Yes">Book 3<BR>
</UL>
<HR>
<input type=submit value="Submit ">
<input type=res
</FORM>
</BODY>
</HTML>
```

Making a few choices

Which book do you want to order?

☒ Book 1
☐ Book 2
☐ Book 3

Submit Clear

Selection Lists

HTML forms offer two more common methods of presenting predetermined choices in addition to radio buttons and check boxes. These are *selection lists*, better known as pop-up menus and scrolling lists.

Pop-up menus allow a person to choose only one item from a list just like radio buttons. The first option listed in the HTML document is the default selection when the form first loads or when the user clicks the reset button. However, you can change the default to an item lower in the list by using the **selected** argument.

Scrolling lists allow a person to choose one or more items from a list. Options are not highlighted when the form first loads or when the user clicks the reset button. However, you can set the default to highlight any item in the list by using the **selected** argument.

The text of each selected option serves as the value for pop-up menus and scrolling lists. The browser sends the name and value for each selected option when the user clicks the submit button in the form.

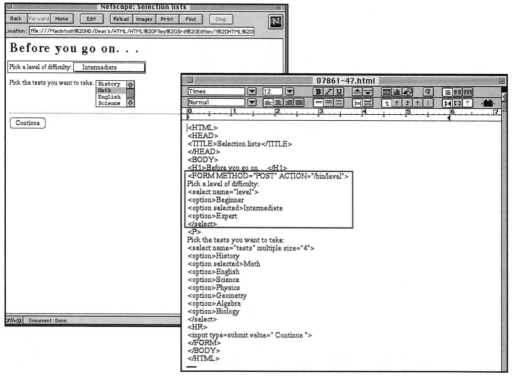

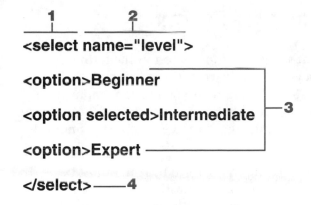

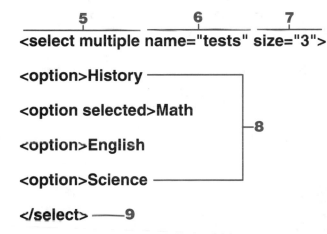

1 Start with the \<select\> tag.

2 Put the name of the pop-up menu between the quote marks.

3 Put the \<option\> tag in front of the text of each item in the pop-up menu. Insert the word selected after \<option\> to change the default to an item lower in the list.

4 End with the \<select\> closing tag.

5 Start with the \<select\> tag. Include multiple for scrolling lists.

6 Put the name of the scrolling list between the quote marks.

7 Put the depth of the scrolling list window between the quote marks.

8 Put the \<option\> tag in front of the text of each item in the scrolling list. Insert the word selected after \<option\> to set the default to highlight any item in the list.

9 End with the \<select\> closing tag.

Graphic Send Buttons in Forms

Every form has a Submit button that sends the information in the form to the server (see page 104). You can use a graphic in place of the standard Submit button by using the **<INPUT TYPE="IMAGE"** tag. This tag inserts a graphic that acts just like a Submit button in that it sends the information in the form to the server. However, it can also act just like an image map (see page 90-93) and link to other files.

The graphic usually presents choices relating to the form but might just be a navigation bar. When the user clicks the graphic, the browser sends the form and the click coordinates to the server for processing. The server's CGI script interprets the click coordinates. This may affect how the information is processed or how it links to other files.

Click coordinates are returned to the server in name value pairs. In the example below, a click at coordinates 20,30 sends **NavigationBar.20** and **whereTo.30** to the server.

1
```
<FORM METHOD="POST" ACTION="/bin/who">
```
2
```
Last name:<INPUT TYPE="text" SIZE="40" NAME="LastName">116
```
3   **4**
```
<INPUT TYPE="IMAGE" SRC="NavigationBar.gif"
NAME="NavigationBar" VALUE="whereTo">
```
5   **7**   **6**
```
<INPUT TYPE="reset" VALUE="clear">
```
8
```
</FORM>
```

1 Start the form with the <FORM> tag (see page 104).

2 Put all the text and input types after the opening tag.

3 Put an image between the quote marks as the input type to create a graphic send button.

4 Use the SRC= argument to insert the graphic and put the name of the graphic file between the quote marks.

5 Choose a name for the graphic send button and put it between the quote marks. This will be attached to the x coordinate of the click.

6 Choose a value for the graphic send button and put it between the quote marks. This will be attached to the y coordinate of the click.

7 Put the copy you want to appear in the reset button between the quote marks.

8 End every form with </FORM>.

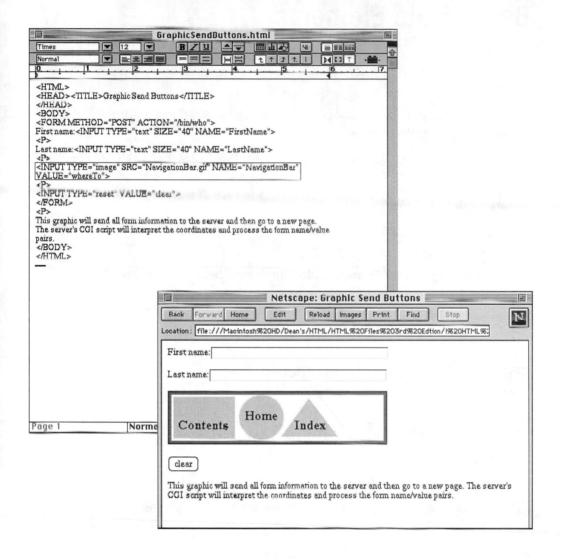

```
<HTML>
<HEAD><TITLE>Graphic Send Buttons</TITLE>
</HEAD>
<BODY>
<FORM METHOD="POST" ACTION="/bin/who">
First name:<INPUT TYPE="text" SIZE="40" NAME="FirstName">
<P>
Last name:<INPUT TYPE="text" SIZE="40" NAME="LastName">
<P>
<INPUT TYPE="image" SRC="NavigationBar.gif" NAME="NavigationBar"
VALUE="whereTo">
<P>
<INPUT TYPE="reset" VALUE="clear">
</FORM>
<P>
This graphic will send all form information to the server and then go to a new page.
The server's CGI script will interpret the coordinates and process the form name/value
pairs.
</BODY>
</HTML>
```

117

Basic Table Elements

A *table* is a special part of the body of an HTML document. Tables organize information in a grid of vertical columns and horizontal rows. Each box is called a *cell*.

Cells can contain text or graphics and other tables. Text and graphics within cells can also be links (see pages 42 and 46).

Tables consist of three basic parts: the caption, headings, and rows of cells. You assemble tables cell by cell, one horizontal row at a time. Start from the top-left corner working your way to the bottom right. Each cell must have something in it. Use a space to create an empty cell.

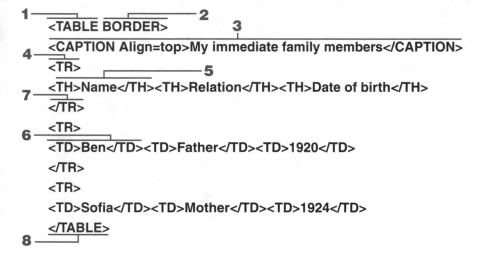

```
<TABLE BORDER>
<CAPTION Align=top>My immediate family members</CAPTION>
<TR>
<TH>Name</TH><TH>Relation</TH><TH>Date of birth</TH>
</TR>
<TR>
<TD>Ben</TD><TD>Father</TD><TD>1920</TD>
</TR>
<TR>
<TD>Sofia</TD><TD>Mother</TD><TD>1924</TD>
</TABLE>
```

1 Start the form with the <TABLE> **tag.**

2 Include BORDER **within the opening tag if you want to have borders around each cell (see page 50).**

3 Put the copy you want to appear as the caption between the <CAPTION> **tags. Captions are optional. Use the** Align **attribute to determine where it appears. Choose** top **or** bottom.

4 Start each row of cells with the <TR> **tag.**

5 Put the copy you want to appear in each heading cell between the <TH> **and** </TH> **tags. Think of TH as meaning table heading.**

6 Put the copy you want to appear in each cell between the <TD> **and** </TD> **tags. Think of TD as meaning table data.**

7 End each row of cells with the </TR> **tag.**

8 End every table with </TABLE>.

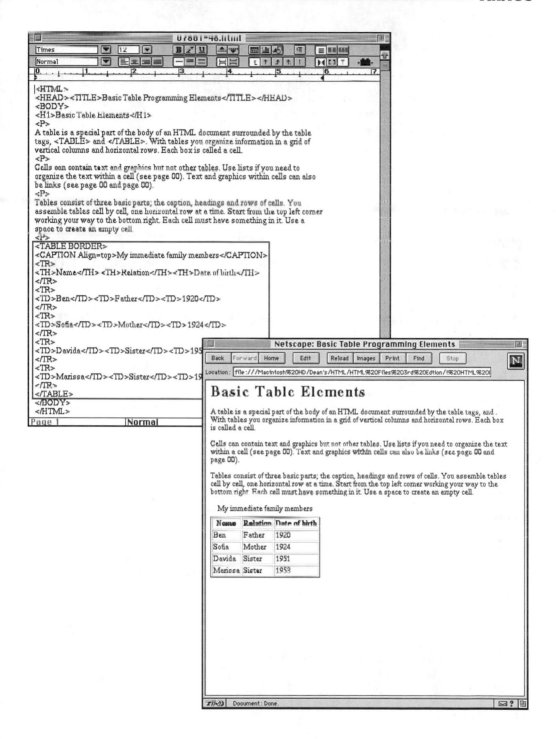

```
<HTML>
<HEAD><TITLE>Basic Table Programming Elements</TITLE></HEAD>
<BODY>
<H1>Basic Table Elements</H1>
<P>
A table is a special part of the body of an HTML document surrounded by the table
tags, <TABLE> and </TABLE>. With tables you organize information in a grid of
vertical columns and horizontal rows. Each box is called a cell.
<P>
Cells can contain text and graphics but not other tables. Use lists if you need to
organize the text within a cell (see page 00). Text and graphics within cells can also
be links (see page 00 and page 00).
<P>
Tables consist of three basic parts; the caption, headings and rows of cells. You
assemble tables cell by cell, one horizontal row at a time. Start from the top left corner
working your way to the bottom right. Each cell must have something in it. Use a
space to create an empty cell.
<P>
<TABLE BORDER>
<CAPTION Align=top>My immediate family members</CAPTION>
<TR>
<TH>Name</TH> <TH>Relation</TH> <TH>Date of birth</TH>
</TR>
<TR>
<TD>Ben</TD><TD>Father</TD><TD>1920</TD>
</TR>
<TR>
<TD>Sofia</TD><TD>Mother</TD><TD>1924</TD>
</TR>
<TR>
<TD>Davida</TD><TD>Sister</TD><TD>195
</TR>
<TR>
<TD>Marissa</TD><TD>Sister</TD><TD>19
</TR>
</TABLE>
</BODY>
</HTML>
```

Page 1   Normal

Netscape: Basic Table Programming Elements

Back | Forward | Home | Edit | Reload | Images | Print | Find | Stop

Location: file:///Macintosh%20HD/Dean's/HTML/HTML%20Files%203rd%20Edtion/!%20HTML%20I

Basic Table Elements

A table is a special part of the body of an HTML document surrounded by the table tags, and .
With tables you organize information in a grid of vertical columns and horizontal rows. Each box
is called a cell.

Cells can contain text and graphics but not other tables. Use lists if you need to organize the text
within a cell (see page 00). Text and graphics within cells can also be links (see page 00 and
page 00).

Tables consist of three basic parts; the caption, headings and rows of cells. You assemble tables
cell by cell, one horizontal row at a time. Start from the top left corner working your way to the
bottom right. Each cell must have something in it. Use a space to create an empty cell.

My immediate family members

Name	Relation	Date of birth
Ben	Father	1920
Sofia	Mother	1924
Davida	Sister	1951
Marissa	Sister	1953

Document: Done.

Spanning Columns and Rows

Cells can span more than one vertical column or horizontal row. You may find it necessary to do this when designing a table. This can also help make information easier to read. Span columns when you want to group cells under a single category or heading. Span rows when information in a cell applies to several horizontal entries.

The **Colspan** and **Rowspan** arguments can be used with **<TH>**, the heading cell tag, and **<TD>**, the table cell tag.

<TABLE BORDER>

<CAPTION Align=top>My immediate family members</CAPTION>

<TR>   1

<TH Colspan=2>Name and Relation</TH><TH>Date of birth</TH>

</TR>

<TR>   2

<TD>Ben</TD><TD Rowspan=2>Parent</TD><TD>1920</TD>

</TR>

<TR>

<TD>Sofia</TD></TD><TD>1924</TD>

</TR>

<TR>

<TD>Davida</TD><TD Rowspan=2>Sister</TD><TD>1951</TD>

</TR>

<TR>

<TD>Marissa</TD><TD>1953</TD>

</TR>

</TABLE>

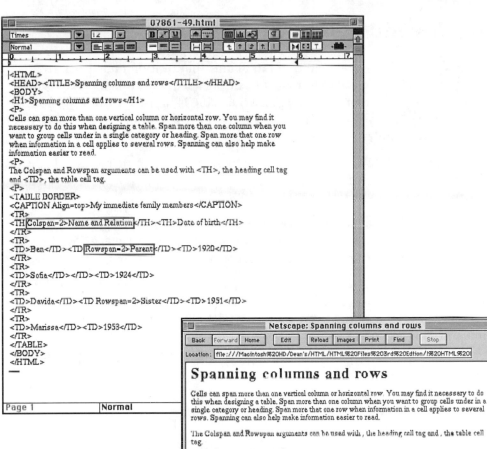

1 Put the Colspan **argument after the** <TH **that starts the cell spanning more than one column. Put the number of columns you want to span after the** = **symbol.**

2 Put the Rowspan **argument after the** <TD **that starts the cell spanning more than one row. Put the number of rows you want to span after the** = **symbol.**

Controlling Width in Tables

You can control the overall width of tables and that of individual cells. In fact, unless you specify width, tables reflow to fit browser windows just like regular text. This may not present a problem if your table is narrow. However, when tables are too wide for the window, they appear on-screen in unacceptable ways. Design and readability may be affected adversely.

You control overall table width two ways: by pixel or percent. Tables will always have the same width when controlled by pixel. Tables will always be the same proportion of window width when controlled by percent.

You control individual cell width two ways as well: by pixel or percent. Cells will always have the same width when controlled by pixel. Cells will always be the same proportion of table width when controlled by percent.

One simple way to handle width is to choose an overall pixel width for the table first and then pick percentages for each column. Percentages, pixel dimensions, and column spanning can affect each other depending on table layout. If you are not getting what you want, look at all these variables. Remember, all rows in a cell will have the same total width. But cells in the same row can have different widths.

```
                               1
                             ┌─────┐
<TABLE BORDER Width=400>
<CAPTION Align=top>My immediate family members</CAPTION>
<TR>                                        2
                                          ┌─────┐
<TH Colspan=2>Name and Relation</TH><TH Width=25%>Date of birth</TH>
</TR>
<TR>
<TD>Ben</TD><TD Rowspan=2>Parent</TD><TD>1920</TD>
</TR>
<TR>
<TD>Sofia</TD></TD><TD>1924</TD>
</TR>
<TR>
<TD>Davida</TD><TD Rowspan=2>Sister</TD><TD>1951</TD>
</TR>
<TR>
<TD>Marissa</TD><TD>1953</TD>
</TR>
</TABLE>
```

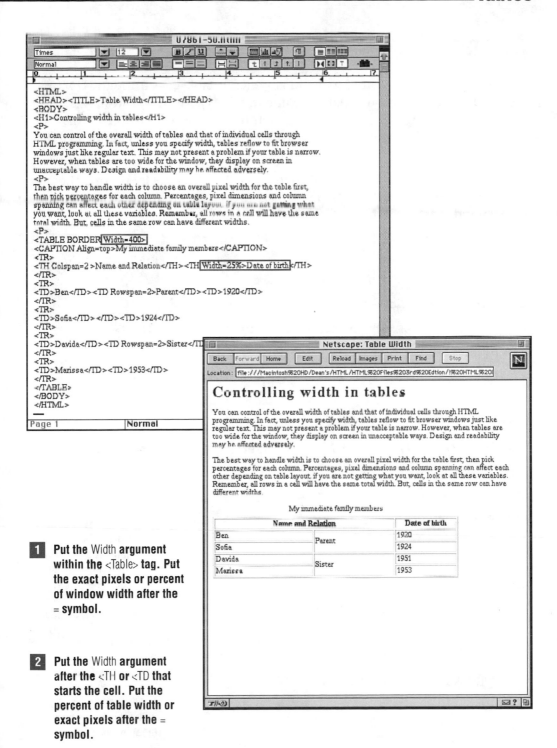

1 Put the Width **argument within the** <Table> **tag. Put the exact pixels or percent of window width after the** = **symbol.**

2 Put the Width **argument after the** <TH **or** <TD **that starts the cell. Put the percent of table width or exact pixels after the** = **symbol.**

Alignment

You can control alignment of text and graphics in table cells through HTML programming. Unless you specify alignment, table captions and headings appear centered, and all other cells align left in the middle of the cell. This looks fine for many tables. However, you may want to improve design and readability through alignment.

You control horizontal and vertical alignment of entire rows by putting the **Align** argument within the **<TR>** tag. You control horizontal and vertical alignment of individual cells by putting the **Align** argument within the **<TH>** or **<TD>** tags.

```
<P>

<TABLE BORDER Width=400>

<CAPTION Align=top>My immediate family members</CAPTION>

<TR Align=Left>        1

<TH Colspan=2 >Name and Relation</TH><TH>Date of birth</TH>

</TR>

<TR >

<TD>Ben</TD><TD Rowspan=2 Align=Center>Parent</TD><TD>1920</TD>

</TR>

<TR>

<TD>Sofia</TD></TD><TD>1924</TD>

</TR>

<TR>

<TD>Davida</TD><TD Rowspan=2 Align=Center
VAlign=top>Sister</TD><TD>1951</TD>
                2
</TR>

<TR>

<TD>Marissa</TD><TD>1953</TD>

</TR>

</TABLE>
```

1 Put the Align **argument within the** <TR> **tag. Put the align option after the** = **symbol. Choose between** Left, Right, **and** Center.

2 Put the VAlign **argument within the** <TH> **or** <TD> **that starts the cell. Put the VAlign option after the** = **symbol. Choose between** Top, Middle, **and** Bottom. **Think of the** V **in** VAlign **as meaning vertical.**

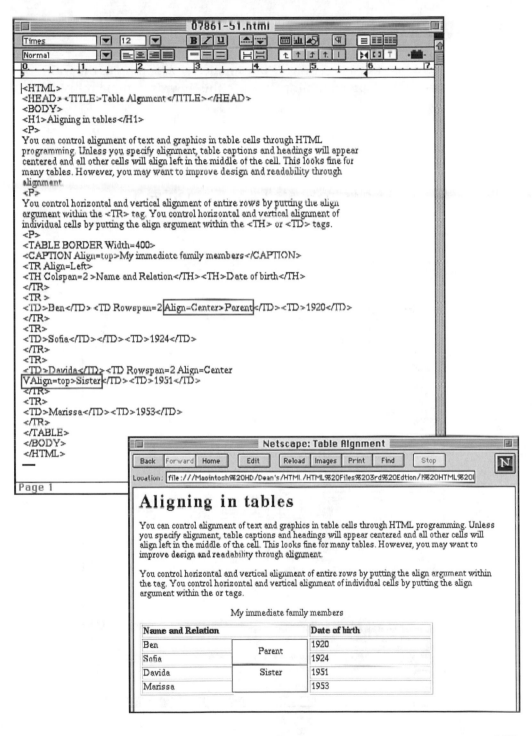

```
<HTML>
<HEAD> <TITLE>Table Alignment</TITLE></HEAD>
<BODY>
<H1>Aligning in tables</H1>
<P>
You can control alignment of text and graphics in table cells through HTML
programming. Unless you specify alignment, table captions and headings will appear
centered and all other cells will align left in the middle of the cell. This looks fine for
many tables. However, you may want to improve design and readability through
alignment.
<P>
You control horizontal and vertical alignment of entire rows by putting the align
argument within the <TR> tag. You control horizontal and vertical alignment of
individual cells by putting the align argument within the <TH> or <TD> tags.
<P>
<TABLE BORDER Width=400>
<CAPTION Align=top>My immediate family members</CAPTION>
<TR Align=Left>
<TH Colspan=2>Name and Relation</TH><TH>Date of birth</TH>
</TR>
<TR >
<TD>Ben</TD> <TD Rowspan=2 Align=Center> Parent</TD><TD>1920</TD>
</TR>
<TR>
<TD>Sofia</TD></TD><TD>1924</TD>
</TR>
<TR>
<TD>Davida</TD><TD Rowspan=2 Align=Center
VAlign=top>Sister</TD><TD>1951</TD>
</TR>
<TR>
<TD>Marissa</TD><TD>1953</TD>
</TR>
</TABLE>
</BODY>
</HTML>
—
```

Page 1

Netscape: Table Alignment

Back | Forward | Home | Edit | Reload | Images | Print | Find | Stop

Location: file:///Macintosh%20HD/Dean's/HTML/HTML%20Files%203rd%20Edtion/!%20HTML%20I

Aligning in tables

You can control alignment of text and graphics in table cells through HTML programming. Unless
you specify alignment, table captions and headings will appear centered and all other cells will
align left in the middle of the cell. This looks fine for many tables. However, you may want to
improve design and readability through alignment.

You control horizontal and vertical alignment of entire rows by putting the align argument within
the tag. You control horizontal and vertical alignment of individual cells by putting the align
argument within the or tags.

My immediate family members

Name and Relation		Date of birth
Ben	Parent	1920
Sofia		1924
Davida	Sister	1951
Marissa		1953

Non-Wrapping Text

You can prevent text in table cells from automatically wrapping to the width of the cell through HTML programming. Just use the **Nowrap** argument inside the **<TD>** tag.

<TD Nowrap>Basic Table Elements</TD>

1 Put the Nowrap **argument within the** <TD> **tag.**

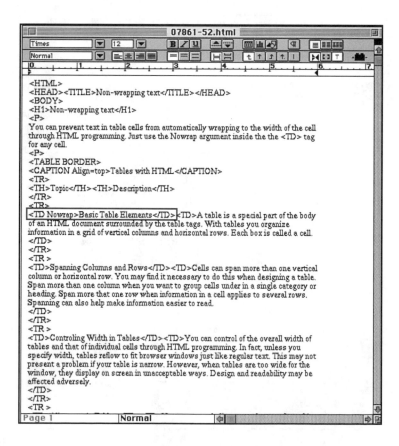

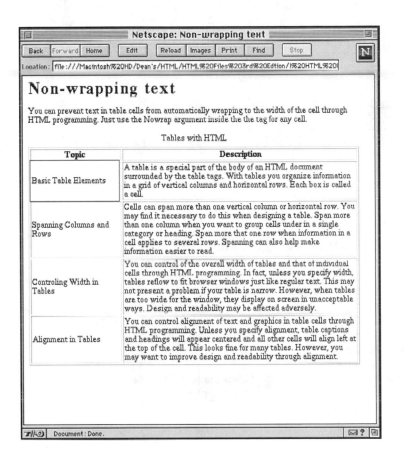

Netscape: Non-wrapping text

Location: file:///Macintosh%20HD/Dean's/HTML/HTML%20Files%203rd%20Edtion/1%20HTML%20|

Non-wrapping text

You can prevent text in table cells from automatically wrapping to the width of the cell through HTML programming. Just use the Nowrap argument inside the the tag for any cell.

Tables with HTML

Topic	Description
Basic Table Elements	A table is a special part of the body of an HTML document surrounded by the table tags. With tables you organize information in a grid of vertical columns and horizontal rows. Each box is called a cell.
Spanning Columns and Rows	Cells can span more than one vertical column or horizontal row. You may find it necessary to do this when designing a table. Span more than one column when you want to group cells under in a single category or heading. Span more that one row when information in a cell applies to several rows. Spanning can also help make information easier to read.
Controling Width in Tables	You can control of the overall width of tables and that of individual cells through HTML. programming. In fact, unless you specify width, tables reflow to fit browser windows just like regular text. This may not present a problem if your table is narrow. However, when tables are too wide for the window, they display on screen in unacceptable ways. Design and readability may be affected adversely.
Alignment in Tables	You can control alignment of text and graphics in table cells through HTML programming. Unless you specify alignment, table captions and headings will appear centered and all other cells will align left at the top of the cell. This looks fine for many tables. However, you may want to improve design and readability through alignment.

Document: Done.

Borders, Spacing, and Padding

You can vary three basic parts of a table that change its look: the border, spacing, and padding. The **BORDER** is the frame outside the table. **Cellspacing** alters the thickness of the grid lines between cells. **Cellpadding** alters the thickness of the empty space between grid lines and text in the cells.

If you don't want any borders, eliminate the **BORDER** argument entirely from the **<TABLE>** tag.

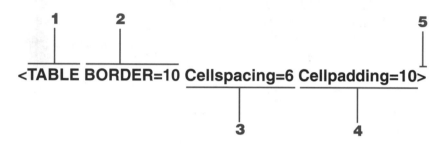

1. Start the table with the <TABLE **tag**.

2. Include BORDER **within the opening tag if you want to have borders around each cell. Put the width of the outside frame measured in pixels after the = symbol.**

3. Include Cellspacing **within the opening tag if you want to alter the grid of lines between cells. Put the width of the grid measured in pixels after the = symbol.**

4. Include Cellpadding **within the opening tag if you want to alter the space between grid lines and text in the cells. Put the width of the space measured in pixels after the = symbol.**

5. Close the table tag with the > symbol.

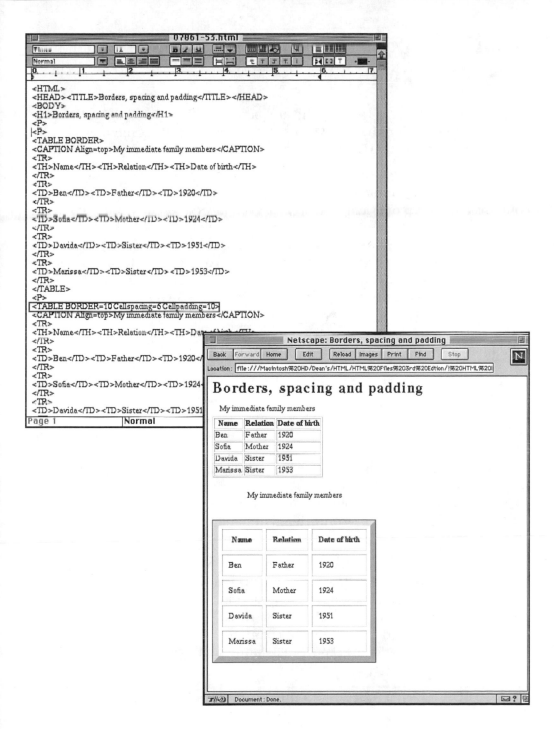

Controlling Grid Lines in Tables with Internet Explorer

A border and grid lines appear around and between cells when the **BORDER=** argument is put within the **<TABLE>** tag (see page 118). With Internet Explorer, you have extra HTML tags that control the border and the grid lines in a variety of ways.

Grid lines help make information more understandable by visually organizing columns and rows. For example, in a table of numbers, you may want to put vertical lines between the columns, but not include horizontal lines. This kind of customized grid improves the table by helping the eye see relationships between the cells. For whatever reason you have, you can elect to draw or erase the border around a table as well as the lines between columns and rows. To change any of these parts, you must first include the **BORDER=** argument within the **<TABLE>** tag.

To alter the border around the table, put the **FRAME=** argument within the **<TABLE>** tag, followed by your choice of the following borders:

BOX draws all four sides of the border.
ABOVE draws only the top of the border.
BELOW draws only the bottom of the border.
HSIDES (Horizontal Sides) draws the horizontal border on the top and bottom of the table.
VSIDES (Vertical Sides) draws the vertical border on the left and right sides of the table.
LHS (Left Hand Side) draws only the left hand side of the border.
RHS (Right Hand Side) draws only the right hand side of the border.
VOID eliminates the border.

To alter the grid lines between columns and rows, put the **RULES=** argument within the **<TABLE>** tag, followed by your choice of grid line options.
ALL draws both vertical and horizontal grid lines.
ROWS draws horizontal grid lines between rows.
COLS draws vertical grid lines between columns.
NONE eliminates all grid lines between columns and rows.

1	2	3	4	5

`<TABLE BORDER=10 FRAME=VOID RULES=ROWS>`

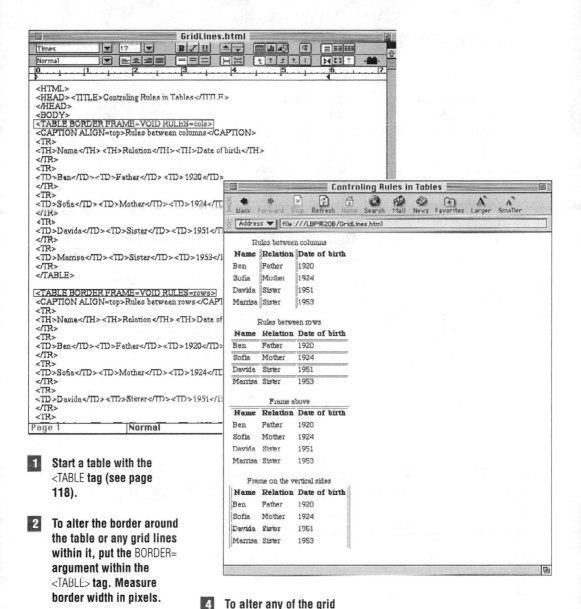

1 Start a table with the <TABLE tag (see page 118).

2 To alter the border around the table or any grid lines within it, put the BORDER= argument within the <TABLE> tag. Measure border width in pixels.

3 To alter the border around the table, put the FRAME= argument within the <TABLE> tag. Choose between BOX, ABOVE, BELOW, HSIDES, VSIDES, LHS, RHS, or VOID.

4 To alter any of the grid lines in the table, put the RULES= argument within the <TABLE> tag. Choose between ALL, ROWS, COLS, or NONE.

5 Close the <TABLE tag with the > symbol.

Using Color in Tables

The color of various parts of a table is controlled with HTML tags. Color can be used to draw attention to specific elements of a table or to enhance the design of a table. For example, in a table of numbers, you may put the bottom row of figures in color to indicate totals for the columns. Or, you may want to alternate colors from row to row for purely aesthetic reasons. Whatever your reason, the background color of a whole table, an entire row, or an individual cell can be specified by using the **BGCOLOR=** argument. To change the color of a whole table's background, put the **BGCOLOR=** argument within the **<TABLE>** tag. To change the color of an entire row, put the **BGCOLOR=** argument within the **<TR>** tag that starts that row. To change the color of an individual cell, put the **BGCOLOR=** argument within the **<TD>** tag of that cell.

Internet Explorer has several more tags for controlling color in tables. All of these tags are placed within the **<TABLE>** tag. However, you must specify a border by using **BORDER=** for any of these tags to have an effect. **BORDER-COLOR=** changes the color of the entire border. Because tables with wide borders have a beveled look, use **BORDERCOLORLIGHT=** to change the color of the light side and **BORDERCOLORDARK=** to change the dark side.

Define the color as either a mix of red, green, and blue or by using one of the standard color names (see page 200).

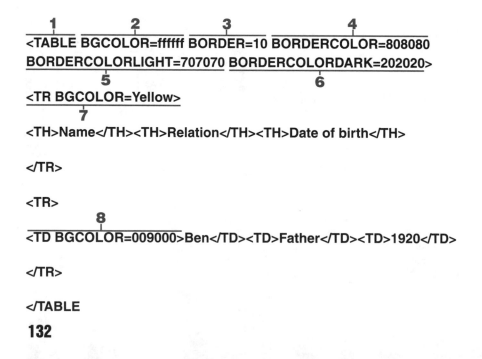

```
                1           2              3                  4
<TABLE BGCOLOR=ffffff BORDER=10 BORDERCOLOR=808080
BORDERCOLORLIGHT=707070 BORDERCOLORDARK=202020>
              5                            6
<TR BGCOLOR=Yellow>
        7
<TH>Name</TH><TH>Relation</TH><TH>Date of birth</TH>

</TR>

<TR>
            8
<TD BGCOLOR=009000>Ben</TD><TD>Father</TD><TD>1920</TD>

</TR>

</TABLE
```

1 Start with the <TABLE> tag to create a table (see page 118).

2 Put the BGCOLOR= argument, followed by the color, within the <TABLE> tag to change the color of a whole table.

3 To create a border for the table, put the BORDER= argument, followed by a number, within the <TABLE> tag. Measure border width in pixels.

4 Put the BORDERCOLOR= argument, followed by either the color mix or color name, within the <TABLE> tag to change the color of a table's border. Internet Explorer only.

5 Put the BORCOLORLIGHT= argument, followed by either the color mix or color name, within the <TABLE> tag to change the color of a light side of the border. Internet Explorer only.

6 Put the BORDERCOLOR-DARK= argument, followed by either the color mix or color name, within the <TABLE> tag to change the color of a dark side of the border. Internet Explorer only.

7 Put the BGCOLOR= argument, followed by either the color mix or color name, within the <TR> tag to change the background color of an entire row.

8 Put the BGCOLOR= argument, followed by either the color mix or color name, within the <TD> tag to change the background color of an individual cell.

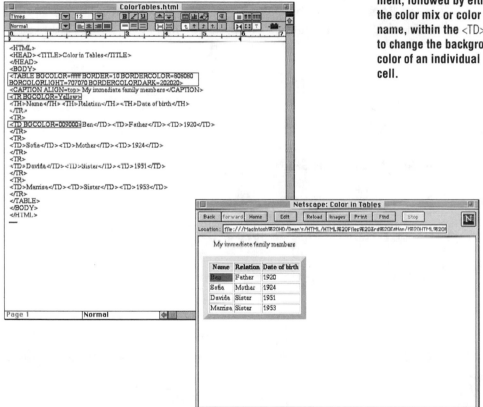

Grouping Columns in Tables with Internet Explorer

Columns of table cells can be grouped by using the **<COLUMN>** tag. This enables you to set cell characteristics that apply to all the cells in a column. This is much easier than setting the style in every cell individually.

Only a few arguments to **<COLUMN>** are currently supported by Internet Explorer. **ALIGN=** shifts the content of the cells to the left, right, or center. **SPAN=** applies the column group to more than one column. Because this tag is useful for controlling cell design, more arguments should be added in the future.

The **<COLUMN>** tag is placed just after the opening **<TABLE>** tag and before any rows are created. Include one **<COLUMN>** tag for each column of cells in the table or use **SPAN=** as described above. If your table has three columns, the first tag effects the right column, the second tag the middle column, and the third tag the right column.

1
<TABLE>

3
<COLGROUP ALIGN=RIGHT>

2—

4 5
<COLGROUP ALIGN=CENTER SPAN=2>

<TR>

<TD>Ben</TD><TD>Father</TD><TD>1920</TD>

</TR>

6—

<TR>

<TD>Sofia</TD><TD>Mother</TD><TD>1924</TD>

</TR>

7
</TABLE>

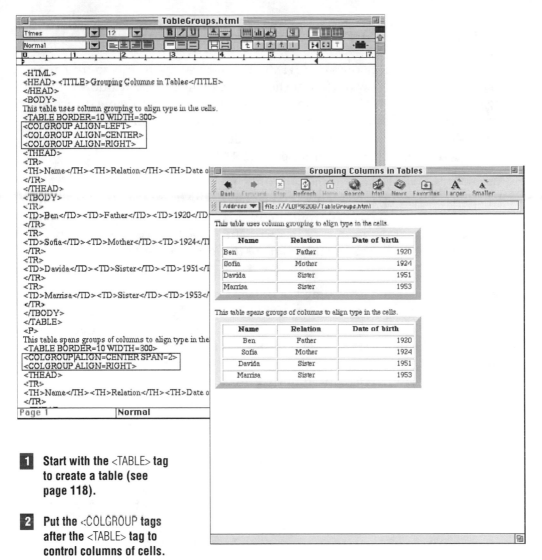

1 Start with the `<TABLE>` tag to create a table (see page 118).

2 Put the `<COLGROUP` tags after the `<TABLE>` tag to control columns of cells.

3 Include `ALIGN=`, followed by the alignment option you want, within the `<COLGROUP` tag. Choose between `LEFT`, `RIGHT`, or `CENTER`.

4 Include `SPAN=` within the `<COLGROUP` tag to group more than one column.

5 Put the number of columns you want to group after the `=` sign.

6 Construct the table row by row (see page 118).

7 Close the table with the `</TABLE>` tag.

What Frames Are and How They Work

One way to display more than one HTML file on a user's screen is to have more than one browser window open. Another way is to divide one window into more than one section. These sections are called frames. Each frame displays a different HTML document and can have its own scroll bars, links, graphics, and so forth. Frames can either function independently or can affect each other by using links that target other frames (see page 144).

To use frames, you need a minimum of three files: a set-up file and two HTML source files. The set-up file describes the layout of the frames within the browser window (see page 142). This file indicates the HTML source files for each frame but contains no text or graphics of its own. The HTML source files are displayed in the frames and, just like any other HTML file, can have links, graphics, tables, and so forth.

Browsers capable of understanding the **<FRAME>** tag read the frame layout as described in the set-up file, then read each HTML source file. The browser displays each source file in the appropriate frame. If the browser is not frame capable, it ignores the **<FRAME>** tag and displays the **<BODY>** of the file, which is usually a message to get a frame capable browser. However, it can be a link to an alternate set of files built for non-frame capable browsers.

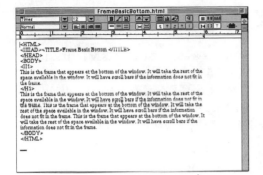

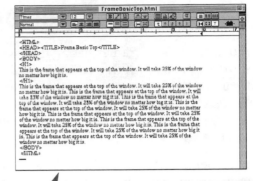

The source files are just like any other HTML file. They contain text, graphics, links, tables, and so forth.

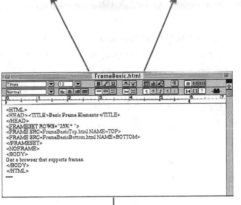

The set-up file describes how the frames section the window and describes the source files for each section.

The browser displays each source file in its own frame within one window.

Basic Frame Elements

A file that sets up frames has all the same elements as any other HTML file. It starts and ends with the **<HTML>** and **</HTML>** tags (see page 20). However, to divide the window into several frames, insert the **<FRAMESET>** tag after the **</HEAD>** tag but before the **<BODY>** of the file. And, to include a message for non-frame capable browsers, put the **<BODY>** of the file within the **<NOFRAME>** tag.

The opening **<FRAMESET>** tag defines the layout of the frames within the browser window. Choose between **COLS** for side-by-side frames or **ROWS** for stacking frames. To divide the window into two sections, include two numbers separated by a comma. To divide the window into three sections, use three numbers separated by a comma, and so on. Measure frame size either in pixels or by percent of window. Use an asterisk (*) if you want the frame size to be whatever remaining space is available. For example, **<FRAMESET COLS="20,50,*">** creates three vertical frames. The left frame measures 20 pixels, the center frame 50 pixels, and the right frame takes up the rest of the window—no matter how large or small it is. If you are using a frame as a graphic navigation bar, you should set the frame to match the size of the graphic. For more on controlling frame layout, see page 142.

After defining the frame layout, you have to fill each frame with an HTML source file. **<FRAME>** tags define the source file for each frame created by the **<FRAMESET>** tag; just put the name of the HTML file within the quote marks after the **SRC=** argument. Each frame should have a name, which is important when targeting frames from links in other frames (see page 144).

<FRAME> tags can contain arguments that control various frame attributes, as listed below.

BORDER= controls the width of the border between frames. Measure border width in pixels.

BORDERCOLOR= controls the color of the border between frames. Color is either a mix of red, green, and blue or a color name (see page 44).

NORESIZE prevents the user from changing the size of frames by dragging their borders. Do not use the **NORESIZE** argument if you want users to be able to resize frames.

SCROLLING= controls whether there are scroll bars on the frame. Just like a browser window, scroll bars will automatically appear on a frame if the source file does not fit. Choose between **YES** or **NO**.

MARGINHEIGHT= adds extra space between the top of the frame and the text or graphics in it. **MARGINWIDTH=** adds extra space between the sides of the frame and the text or graphics. Measure height and width in pixels.

The HTML source files are placed in the frame layout in the order they are listed in the set-up file. For example, if the set-up file defines three vertical frames of different widths, **<FRAMESET COLS="100,200,300">**, and then lists three source files **<FRAME SRC="A.html">**, **<FRAME SRC="B.html">**, and **<FRAME SRC="C.html">**, the left frame, which is 100 pixels wide, will contain file A.html; the center frame, which is 200 pixels wide, will contain file B.html; and the right frame, which is 300 pixels wide, will contain file C.html.

```
            1           2        3
<FRAMESET COLS="40%,*">
      4         5                      6
<FRAME SRC="A.html" NAME="StuffOnTheLEFT"

BORDER=10 BORDERCOLOR="202020"

NORESIZE SCROLLING=YES
                            8
MARGINHEIGHT=20 MARGINWIDTH=30>

<FRAME SRC="B.html" NAME="StuffOnTheRIGHT">
      10
</FRAMESET>

<NOFRAME>

<BODY>

Get a browser that supports frames.

</BODY>

</NOFRAME>
```

1 Start with the <FRAMESET tag.

2 Within the <FRAMESET> tag, put COLS= for vertical frames or ROWS= for horizontal frames, followed by dimensions for each frame. Separate the dimensions by commas. Measure either in pixels or by percent of window. Use an asterisk (*) if you want the frame size to be whatever remaining space is available.

3 Close the <FRAMESET tag with the > symbol.

4 Include a <FRAME> tag for each frame defined by the <FRAMESET> tag.

5 Put the name of the HTML file for each frame within the quote marks after the SRC= argument.

6 Put the name of each frame within the quote marks after the NAME= argument.

7 Include any other frame attributes you want to control within the <FRAME> tag. (see page 138)

8 Close the <FRAME tag with the > symbol.

9 List other <FRAME> tags in order between the <FRAMESET> and </FRAMESET> tags.

10 Close the <FRAMESET> tag with the </FRAMESET> tag.

11 Put a message for non-frame capable browsers as the body of the file between the <NOFRAME> and </NOFRAME> tags.

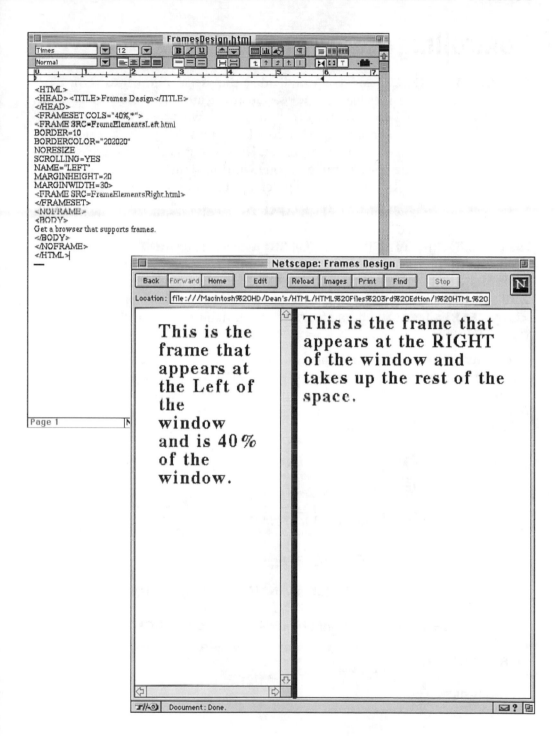

Controlling Frame Layout

With the **<FRAMESET>** tag, you can divide a browser window into vertical or horizontal frames. Frames placed side-by-side are created with the **COLS=** argument. Frames stacked one over the other are created with the **ROWS=** argument. Often, browser windows are composed of only side-by-side or stacked frames. This works fine for many Web sites. However, it is also possible to mix both stacked and side-by-side frames in one window. This is done by nesting **<FRAMESET>** tags. In other words, you can put frames inside frames.

In the example below, the first **<FRAMESET>** tag divides the window into two equal frames, stacked one over the other. Next, using the **<FRAME>** tag, it fills the top half with an HTML source file, **SRC="FrameLayoutTop.html"**. Then, instead of filling the bottom half with a second **<FRAME>** tag and source file, it is again divided in half with a new **<FRAMESET>** tag. This, in turn, gets filled with two **<FRAME>** source files. If you're confused, just think of the second **<FRAMESET>** tag as the filling for the bottom half of the first **<FRAMESET>** tag.

This is just one way of nesting frames to divide a browser window. Try other layouts that fit your needs. But make sure each **<FRAMESET>** tag is closed with its own matching **</FRAMESET>** tag. Also, remember to keep track of the frames by name in case you need to target any one of these frames with a link from another frame (see page 144).

```
                1              2          3
<FRAMESET ROWS="50%,50%">
                               4                          5
<FRAME SRC="FrameLayoutTop.html" NAME="TOP">
                    6
<FRAMESET COLS="50%,50%">

<FRAME SRC="FrameLayoutLeft.html" NAME="BottomLEFT">
7-                                                         -8
<FRAME SRC="FrameLayoutRight.html" NAME="BottomRIGHT">

</FRAMESET>
9-
</FRAMESET>
```

1. **Start with the** <FRAMESET tag.

2. **Within the** <FRAMESET> tag, put COLS= for vertical frames or ROWS= for horizontal frames, followed by dimensions for each frame. Separate the dimensions by commas. Measure either in pixels or by percent of window. Use an asterisk (*) if you want the frame size to be the remaining available space.

3. **Close the** <FRAMESET tag with the > symbol.

4. **Include a** <FRAME> tag for each frame defined by the <FRAMESET> tag. Put the name of the HTML file for each frame within the quote marks after the SRC= argument. Make sure you name each frame with the NAME= argument.

5. **Close the** <FRAME tag with the > symbol.

6. **Divide the frame again** with a second <FRAMESET tag.

7. **Include a** <FRAME> tag for each frame defined by the second <FRAMESET> tag. Put the name of the HTML file for each frame within the quote marks after the SRC= argument. Make sure you name each frame with the NAME= argument.

8. **Close the** <FRAME tag with the > symbol.

9. **Close each** <FRAMESET> tag with its matching </FRAMESET> tag.

Targeting Frames with Links

Targeting is a way of making links in one frame change the file displayed in another frame. Navigation bars are one common use for targets. A navigation bar appears in a non-scrolling frame at the top, bottom, or to one side of the window. It contains a set of links that cause different files to be displayed in a second, usually larger, frame. This is done by stating the target frame as part of the link. The link can be simple text, a graphic, or an image map.

It takes two parts to make a target work properly. First, when creating the frame in the set-up file, you must name it. Then, when creating the link, you must use that same name to indicate in which frame the linked HTML file should be displayed.

The set-up file:

1

```
<FRAMESET COLS="25%,*">

<FRAME SRC="firstFrameBasic.html" NAME="LEFT">
                                    3
<FRAME SRC="secondFrameNew.html" NAME="RIGHT">

</FRAMESET>
```
2

The link:

5

```
<A HREF="SecondFrameNew.html" TARGET="RIGHT">

See something new</A>
```
4

---

1 Start with the <FRAMESET tag to divide the window into frames (see page 138).

2 Include a <FRAME> tag for each frame defined by the <FRAMESET> tag. Put the name of the HTML file for each frame within the quote marks after the SRC= argument.

3 Name each frame with the NAME= argument so that you can target the frame with a link.

4 Create a link with the <A HREF tag (see page 52).

5 Include the TARGET= argument within the link. Put the name of the frame between the quote marks as the target frame.

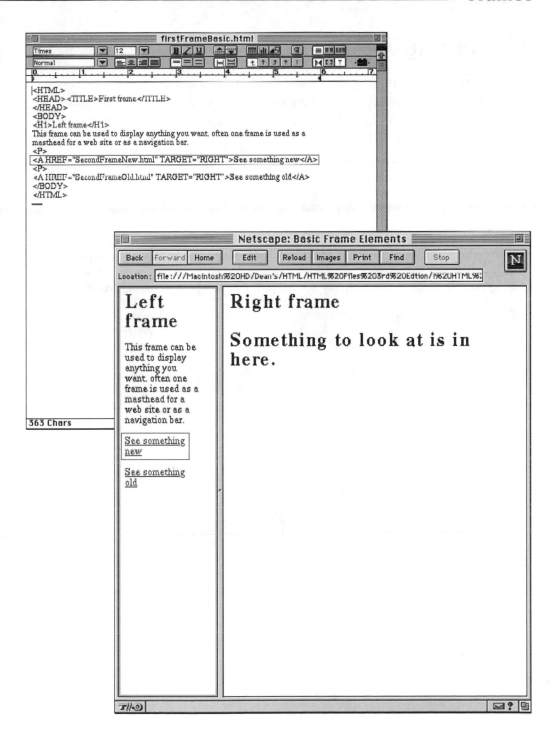

Home Pages

The first HTML document that you want people to see when they get to your Web site is called a *home page.* Home pages set the tone for the rest of your pages. Whether you design splashy or purely functional home pages, they should include certain elements.

Good home pages describe the service the site provides or tell the user what information is available on the site. They instruct new users about unique features or software that is needed. They include an address for feedback. How you accomplish this is your decision.

Splashy home pages have big graphics. Sometimes large image maps act as navigation for the document as a whole. Others have graphic navigation bars that repeat on every page. Remember, big graphics mean your home page will take a long time to transfer over the Web. A first-time user may cancel before the page ever loads.

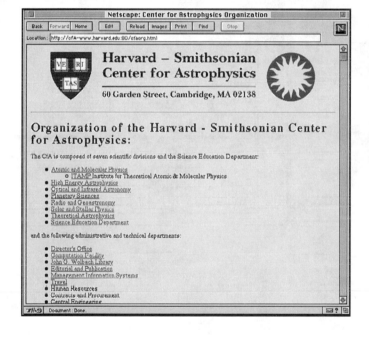

Table of contents-style home pages rely heavily on linked text. Sometimes small graphics accompany the text. Everyone knows how to use a table of contents, so there is no learning curve for this type of page. Using text exclusively means your home page will take the shortest time possible to transfer over the Web.

Structuring Multi-Page Documents— Linear

One way to present information is with a *linear structure*. A person moves forward or back through files just like turning pages in a book. One HTML file follows the next. Each HTML file includes a link to the next and preceding files. You determine the order in which the information is presented.

You do not need to make a diagram of linear documents; these documents do not have complicated connections to keep track of. Just remember to check the URLs in the links to the next and preceding files when you add or remove a file in the structure.

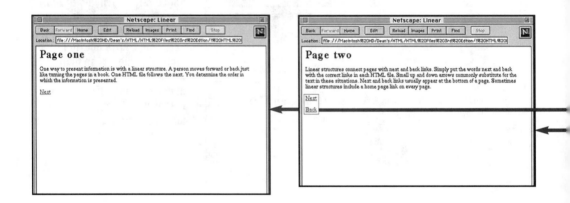

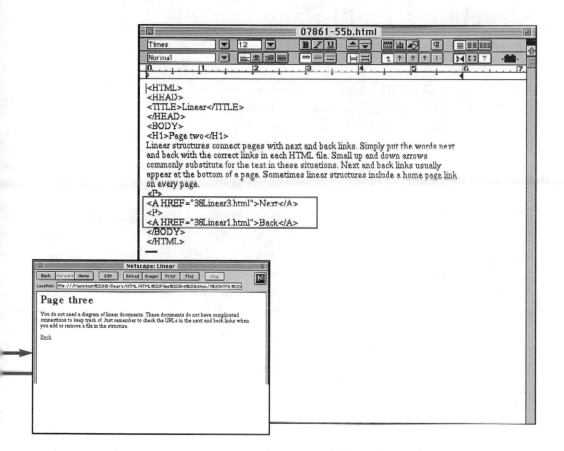

```
<HTML>
<HEAD>
<TITLE>Linear</TITLE>
</HEAD>
<BODY>
<H1>Page two</H1>
Linear structures connect pages with next and back links. Simply put the words next
and back with the correct links in each HTML file. Small up and down arrows
commonly substitute for the text in these situations. Next and back links usually
appear at the bottom of a page. Sometimes linear structures include a home page link
on every page.
<P>
<A HREF="38Linear3.html">Next</A>
<P>
<A HREF="38Linear1.html">Back</A>
</BODY>
</HTML>
```

Page three

You do not need a diagram of linear documents. These documents do not have complicated
connections to keep track of. Just remember to check the URLs in the next and back links when
you add or remove a file in the structure.

Back

Linear structures connect pages with next and back links. Simply put the words Next and Back with the correct links in each HTML file. Small up and down arrows commonly substitute for the text in these situations. Next and back links usually appear at the bottom of a page. Sometimes linear structures include a home page link on every page.

Structuring Multi-Page Documents—Non-Linear

One way to present information is with a *non-linear structure*, in which a person jumps between interconnected pages. One HTML file relates to many others like a three-dimensional maze. The person viewing your documents determines the order in which the information is presented from the possibilities you provide.

Non-linear structures connect pages with hypertext links. Simply put as many text and graphic links in each HTML file as you want. Home page links usually appear at the bottom of each page. Sometimes non-linear structures include linear sections.

Draw a diagram of non-linear documents. Even simple documents have many connections to keep track of. A diagram helps you keep track of all the files and links, making updates easier. When you remove pages, you're less likely to overlook important links if you have a good diagram.

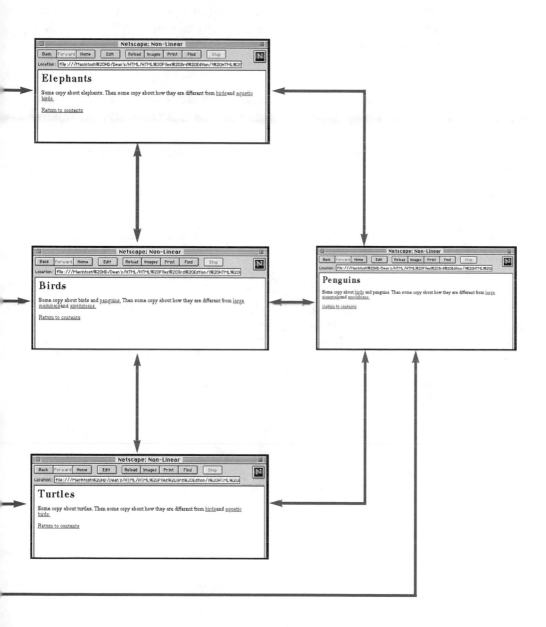

Navigation

Navigation within and between HTML files is important. If you provide good navigation, people will find it easy to use your service or purchase your products. Think about the basic mechanisms needed to get around the files, but also think about what makes them easier to use.

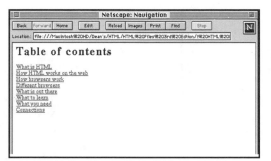

A table of contents is one of the most common means of navigation. Each item in the table of contents links to another HTML file or to an anchor in the same file. A person reads through the topics, jumps quickly to one of interest, and then returns to the contents.

Simple paging (or a linear structure, see page 148) takes little advantage of the hypertext capabilities of HTML. One HTML file follows the next just like the pages in a book. There are times when this makes good sense. For example, no one gets lost in a maze of information when paging.

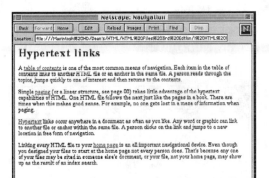

Hypertext links can occur anywhere in a document as often as you like. Any word or graphic can link to another file or anchor within the same file. A person clicks on the link and jumps to a new location in a free form of navigation.

Linking every HTML file to your home page is an all-important navigational device. Even though you designed your files to start at the home page, not every person will start there. That's because any one of your files may be cited in someone else's document, or your file, not your home page, may show up as the result of an index search.

Navigational Aids

People need help keeping track of where they are in the maze of information you can create with hypertext links. They also like Web documents to be easy to use. Some simple navigational aids can help on both accounts. These are in addition to basic navigation provided by things like a table of contents, simple paging, hypertext, and links to home pages, as discussed on the previous pages.

Clear headings help people know what they are looking at. When properly worded, headings concisely describe a file's content or function. Some headings describe how the current file relates to the whole document.

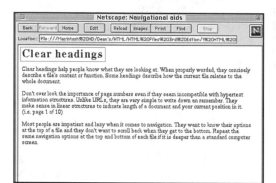

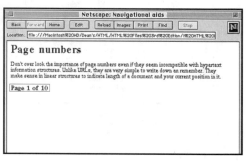

Clear, concise headings communicate quickly, allowing a person to decide whether to stop or go on.

Page numbers give a person a sense of place within a large document.

Don't overlook the importance of page numbers, even if they seem incompatible with hypertext information structures. Unlike URLs, page numbers are very simple to write down and remember. They make sense in linear structures to indicate the length of a document and your current position in it (for example, page 1 of 10).

Most people are impatient and lazy when it comes to navigation. They want to know their options at the top of a file, and they don't want to scroll back when they get to the bottom. Repeat the same navigation options at the top and bottom of each file if it is longer than a standard computer screen.

Navigation options at the top of a file avoid having to hunt for options within the text.

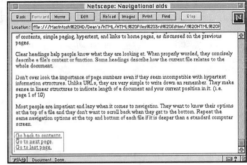

Navigation options at the bottom of a file provide logical next steps in the information flow.

Design Issues

Design on the Web means two things: structural information design and graphic design. The previous pages cover some basic structural design issues and suggest techniques for organizing the information. Other books go into greater depth than this book has space for.

When it comes to graphic design, electronic publishing with HTML is similar to desktop publishing. Software, however, does not make you a designer; if you know you are bad at design, don't try. Hire help. Stick with text. Keep it simple.

If you can design, knock yourself out. Remember that a few factors remain out of your control.

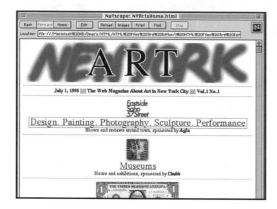

The available fonts and typestyle preferences on the user's computer can differ from those on your screen.

This is the same file as that on the left, viewed with different font preferences.

A rescaled browser window can crop graphics and rewrap text, causing different line breaks. Graphics meant to appear together on one line may stack instead.

Long load times for those big graphics you spent hours on can cause people to cancel before they reach your page. Also, keep in mind that some people on the Web browse with the image loading turned off.

Beyond Design

The reason for any HTML document is the information, product, or service it provides. The text, graphics, sound, and video files all support that goal—they make it useful, easy, clear, and convenient. Sometimes the right text in the right place accomplishes this in a big way.

Include notes on external files. For FTP links, include file sizes. This helps the user estimate how long transfers will take. People can decide if they really want the file and then decide when to schedule a download and how to make room on their hard disk. For sound and video, include the format and file size (see page 86).

Date your file in the text, just like newspapers or letters, so that people can tell at a glance if they've already read the file. Or include a "what's new" page for each update.

Leave behind a pointer page when you change your URL. It is just like getting a recorded message when someone changes their phone number. Pointer pages don't have to be pretty, just effective. At the old address, provide the new address along with any important messages. Include links to URLs that people expect to find, as well as related URLs.

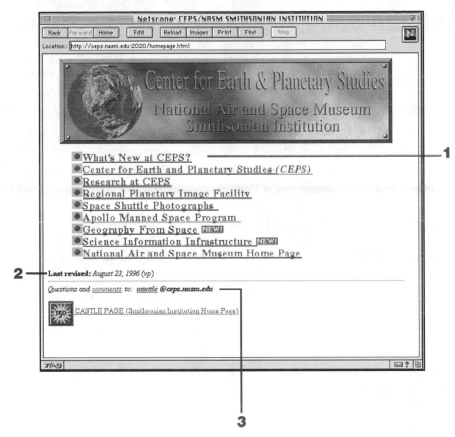

1 A "what's new" link gives people a quick way of skimming the current document highlights.

2 Dating the file in the text tells people at-a-glance if they have read it already.

3 E-mail links are a convenient feature in some browsers.

Comments in Programming

You can insert lines of text in your HTML files that browsers will not display; these are called *comments*. Comments allow you to annotate your HTML programming so that your notes remain a part of the file itself. Every line of a comment begins with the **<!** tag and ends with the **>** tag. Do not use any other tags inside comments, as these will confuse some browsers that display the comment instead of ignoring it.

Use a comment when you want to remember something special about your file, for example, why you used certain URLs or gateway scripts.

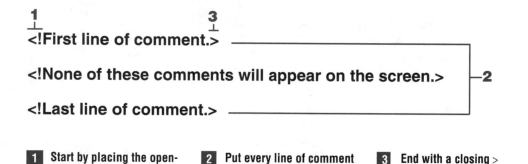

1 Start by placing the opening <! tag in front of the comment.

2 Put every line of comment between its own comment tags.

3 End with a closing > symbol after every line of comment.

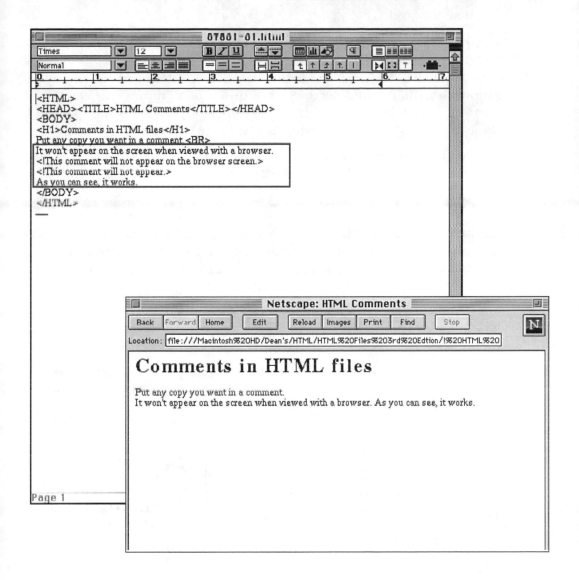

```
<HTML>
<HEAD><TITLE>HTML Comments</TITLE></HEAD>
<BODY>
<H1>Comments in HTML files</H1>
Put any copy you want in a comment <BR>
It won't appear on the screen when viewed with a browser.
<!This comment will not appear on the browser screen.>
<!This comment will not appear.>
As you can see, it works.
</BODY>
</HTML>
```

Netscape: HTML Comments

Back | Forward | Home | Edit | Reload | Images | Print | Find | Stop

Location: file:///Macintosh%20HD/Dean's/HTML/HTML%20Files%203rd%20Edtion/!%20HTML%20

Comments in HTML files

Put any copy you want in a comment.
It won't appear on the screen when viewed with a browser. As you can see, it works.

Page 1

161

Consistency in Programming

You should format HTML word processing files in a consistent and logical way for your own benefit, not for the browser's. Browsers don't notice how you format your files, they only notice the tags. They ignore extra returns and spaces unless you tag the copy as preformatted text (see page 82).

Whether you type one continuous line of code or put a return after every word, both documents look the same when browsed as long as the content is identical.

Whenever possible, format the file so that it mimics the look of the browsed file. This makes it easier to visualize the browser page and find mistakes. Isolate key elements on separate lines so that you can check them at a glance. Find a consistent way of formatting files that makes sense to you and stick with it.

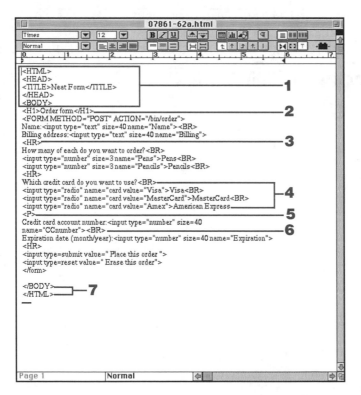

1 Put each tag in the HTML header at the top on a line of its own.

2 Put elements like headings on lines of their own.

3 Put rules on their own lines.

4 Use the identical order for arguments of each radio button, check box, and selection list. Put every item on its own line.

5 Put paragraph breaks on their own line so that they look like the line space they create.

6 Put line breaks at the end of the line where they perform their functions.

7 Put each tag in the HTML footer at the bottom on a line of its own.

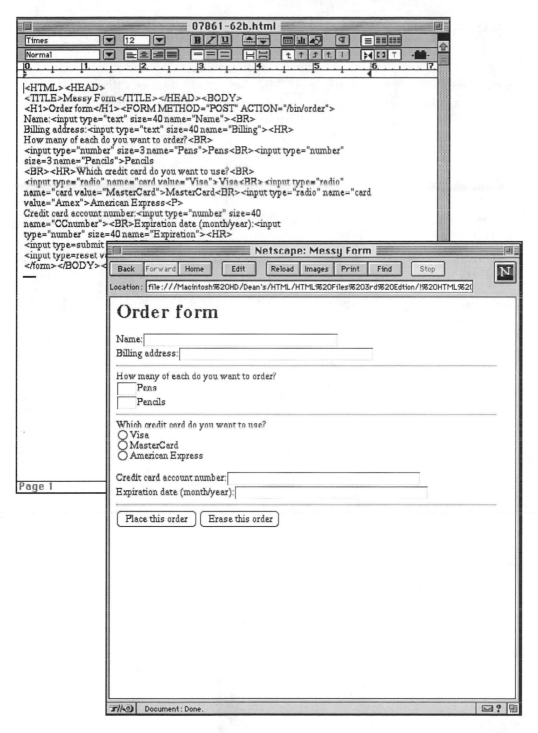

Testing

Before posting any pages, you have to test them. Programming is inherently buggy even when it is as simple as HTML. You should test your files locally and keep them all on your own hard disk off any network before you post them on the Web. View them with several different browsers, not just your favorite one. You will discover differences that may be important enough to warrant changes.

Besides the obvious examples on the next page, make sure you check the following list. Keep in mind, though, that many of these items are difficult—if not impossible—to check until the HTML files are posted on the Web server. You can arrange to post pages that require a password for viewing so that you can test everything before it is made public.

- *Spelling.* Spell check the file or ask someone else to proofread the screen for you.

- *Navigation.* Make sure every page has the necessary navigation and that it works correctly.

- *External files.* Place graphic, sound, and video files where they can be found and loaded. Include alternate text for non-graphical browsers.

- *Load times.* Are they acceptable or are they too long?

- *Forms.* Do the gateway scripts work properly?

- *Dummy test.* Have someone new to the document run through it; something is bound to turn up that you never noticed.

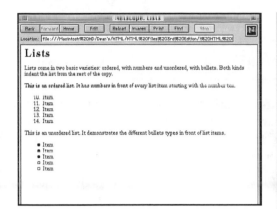

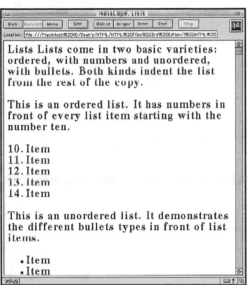

In this example, a missing closing tag for a heading drastically changed the look of the browsed file. The heading style remained in effect for the rest of the text.

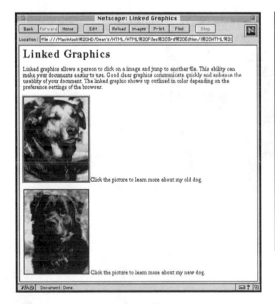

In this example, a misplaced graphic file or incorrect URL stopped the browser from loading one image.

Posting Pages

No one will see your HTML files unless you post them (make them accessible) on a server in a network.

You can post files on a server in a closed network, like one at work, if you want to restrict viewing to people in that network. Or you can make your HTML documents available to everyone browsing the Web by placing them on an Internet server. Some Internet servers also restrict access to files. For example, you may have to subscribe or obtain special clearance.

Send your HTML, graphic, sound, and video files along with any gateway scripts to the server. You can do this over the Internet or by sending a disk to the server administrator. Use the method the administrator prefers.

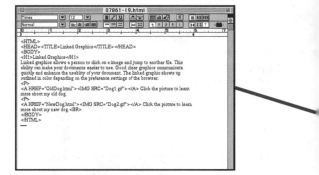

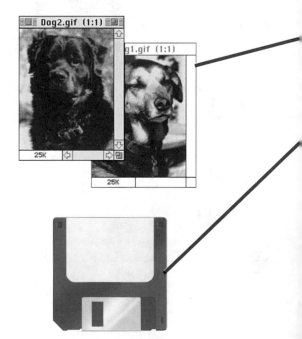

The people operating the server you work with govern how you post pages to the server. If they like do-it-yourselfers and your files are small, you can probably transfer them over the Internet. Otherwise, you just send a disk and the system administrator does the rest. It's a very good idea to recheck all of the links, scripts, etc., to be sure they all work as soon as the pages are posted.

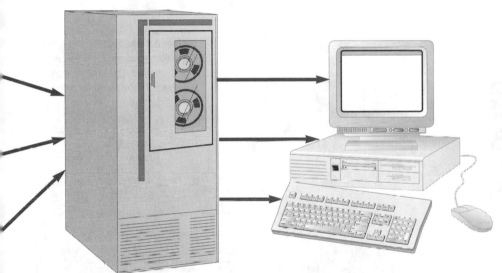

The server holds all your files and gateway scripts on a hard disk and makes the files available to Web browsers. It runs your gateway scripts and returns the results. Internet servers make files available over the high-speed data lines to other Internet servers and to computers with modems over dial-up connections.

Many individuals browsing the Web can view your HTML documents at the same time when they are placed on an Internet server. Each computer requests a file from the server by using its URL address.

Finding a Server

New Internet servers are popping up all over; you don't have to look very hard to find one these days. Most large corporations, government agencies, research institutes, and colleges and universities have servers. If not, they are most likely planning to set one up in the near future.

Check for a server where you work or study before you search for a commercial server for your files. It could be available to you free of charge. Ask the network administrator if you can use it.

To find a commercial server, start by asking friends and colleagues. Someone you know probably researched the topic recently and can save you time. If not, surf the Web and look for e-mail addresses of the commercial servers. See page 174 for a short list that can get you started.

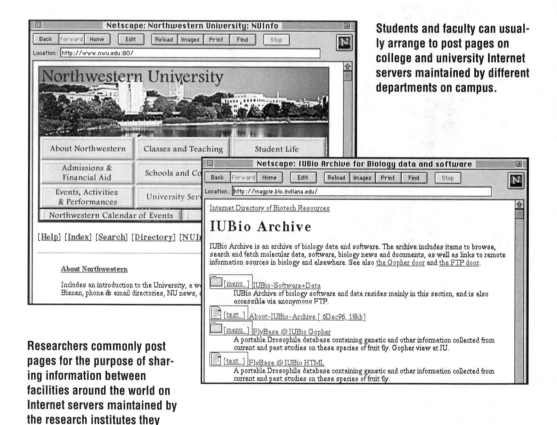

Students and faculty can usually arrange to post pages on college and university Internet servers maintained by different departments on campus.

Researchers commonly post pages for the purpose of sharing information between facilities around the world on Internet servers maintained by the research institutes they work for.

Employees may work for a company with an Internet server of its own. However, corporations operate these servers for business and tightly control who and what gets posted.

Civil servants may work for a government agency with an Internet server of its own. You cannot use it for private purposes.

Commercial servers offer access accounts for all Internet services and provide space to post Web pages. Fees and rates vary.

Should You Set Up Your Own Server?

In the past, setting up an Internet server has been a big undertaking. The hardware and software were complex and required significant technical expertise. They also cost a lot of money.

It's no longer true that a server will be prohibitively expensive. Relatively inexpensive all-in-one Web servers are now available that come bundled with hardware and software. But, don't underestimate the money required to connect to the Internet with a dedicated line.

Until recently, individuals and small businesses have not considered setting up a server; it has been just as easy to rent space from a commercial server. However, many individuals are now setting up servers due to dropping costs.

Groups that should consider setting up a server include the organizations like those that you see on the Web already: corporations, schools, museums, and research institutes. They tend to be large and have equally large capital expenditure budgets for computer equipment each year. Commercial enterprises that expect significant income from Web services should consider setting up a server.

Are you considering setting up your own server? If your answer to these questions is more often no than yes, consider space on a commercial server instead of setting up your own.

Historically, servers operated on a UNIX system had full-time system administrators. Recently, there's been a flood of PC and Macintosh software for this. There are several servers that individuals might use for Windows for a simple Web site. Windows NT is fast becoming the platform of choice for new Web servers in corporate settings.

	Yes	No
Is Web publishing the best way to distribute your information?	☐	☐
Is a server part of a long-range strategy for your organization?	☐	☐
Does your organization need control of the server for security reasons?	☐	☐
Do you have the equipment and software already?	☐	☐
Do you have the know-how to set up and maintain a server?	☐	☐
Do you have the time it takes to be a system administrator or do you have a full-time system administrator on staff?	☐	☐
Can you afford to hire a full-time system administrator?	☐	☐
Do you need to have a programmer for the server you set up?	☐	☐
Can you program or do you have a programmer for the UNIX platform?	☐	☐
Do you have or can you afford a high-speed connection to the Internet?	☐	☐
Do you know all the costs involved?	☐	☐
Can you afford all the costs involved?	☐	☐

Setting Up Your Own Server

Once you decide to set up your own server, you need to design a system that meets your needs. There are more and more companies that sell out-of-the-box hardware and software systems at affordable prices. Sales representatives are eager to help.

Local telephone companies provide connections to the Internet. They sell or rent equipment that interfaces their line with your network. Shop around; your local baby bell isn't usually the cheapest source. T1 lines are the most common connections. They are reasonably fast for the money. An ISDN line provides an inexpensive alternative if you use the line for only a part of the day and don't expect a high volume of traffic. You pay a monthly fee for the line and a rate for timed usage.

If you are interested in running a simple server for yourself or a small company, you should look at the book *Running a Perfect Web Site, Second Edition*, by Stephen Wynkoop. It includes a CD-ROM with server software for several platforms.

Ask yourself these questions:

- Do you want a Web server or a full-featured Internet server that includes other Internet services, like e-mail and Gopher? You can get a cheap e-mail account at a local access provider rather than setting up a mail server of your own.

- Do you need to transact business or is the server for purely informational needs? Secure systems cost more.

- How fast a transmission line do you need? Higher speed equals higher cost.

- What platform should you operate? Choose one that makes sense in your LAN.

A server begins the list of equipment you need. You will want to get a fast one with expandable memory and the capability of attaching multiple hard disks. You may also need a *router,* which manages the flow of data from other nodes on the Internet. It receives packets of information from other servers, reads the URLs, and sends them on to their destinations.

A system administrator will set up the server, maintain it, update software, troubleshoot problems, and manage file transfers.

Short List of Commercial Servers

There are hundreds, perhaps thousands, of companies selling their services as commercial Web servers. Here are just a few of them. Most of these servers are large national service providers. You may also find local providers in your area. Some of these providers also provide their services as Web authors and designers if you need to outsource that work.

Server	URL
Atlantic	http://www.atlantic.com/
Aztec Internet Services	http://www.aztec.com/pub/aztec/
Branch Information Services	http://branch.com/
Catalog.Com	http://www.catalog.com/catalog/top.html
CERFnet	http://www.cerfnet.com/
CommerceNet CyberGate, Inc.	http://www.commerce.net/
Cybersight Services	http://www.cybersight.com/
Digital Marketing, Inc.	http://www.digimark.net/
Digital Planet	http://www.digiplanet.com/
Downtown Anywhere	http://www.awa.com/
EarthLink Network	http://www.earthlink.net/
ElectriCiti	http://www.electriciti.com/
Electric Press, Inc.	http://www.elpress.com/
Great Lakes Area Commercial Internet	http://www.glaci.com/
Home Pages, Inc.	http://www.homepages.com/
Internet Distribution Services	http://www.service.com/
ECHO	http://www.imperative.com/
Internet Information Systems	http://www.internet-is.com/
HoloNet	http://www.holonet.com/
IQuest Network Services	http://www.iquest.net/
NetCenter	http://netcenter.com/

NETCOM	**http://www.netcom.com/netcom/ prodserv.html**
NetMarket	**http://netmarket.com/nm/ pages/home**
New Jersey Computer Connection	**http://www.njcc.com/**
The Pipeline	**http://www.pipeline.com/**
Primenet	**http://com.primenet.com/ featured.html**
PSINet	**http://www.psi.net/**
QuakeNet	**http://www.quake.net**
Quantum Networking Solutions	**http://www.gcr.com**
The SEAMLESS WEBSite	**http://seamless.com/ chambers.html**
The Sphere	**http://www.thesphere.com/**
SSNet	**http://ssnet.com/**
Stelcom	**http://www.webscope.com/**
Streams Online Media Development	**http://streams.com/**
Televisions, Inc.	**http://www.tvisions.com/**
The Tenagra Corporation	**http://arganet.tenagra.com/**
TurnPike Metropolis	**http://turnpike.net/turnpike/ metro.html**
World Wide Access	**http://www.wwa.com/wwa.html**
Z-Depth	**http://www.zdepth.com/**
WinNET	**http://www.win.net**

Costs

Servers are definitely in business to make money. They do this through service fees, monthly rates, and commissions. Charges vary widely from server to server. You will not necessarily encounter all three costs at every server. Call a few to compare pricing and ask a lot of questions. Try to negotiate a better deal, if you can.

Large servers offer turnkey solutions. Staff programmers and designers do everything for you. You can also hire freelance programmers and designers at reasonable hourly rates.

Most servers charge setup fees when you first post your pages. The fees can cover programming that enables the server to track usage and generate reports that tell you how many people look at which pages each month. Additional fees are charged for any work that you ask the server to do for you, such as programming or screen design.

Servers may charge monthly rates for keeping your files posted. Some ask you to commit for a three-month minimum to start. They base their rates on the megabytes of hard disk space you require and the megabytes viewed per month. If you are in a retail business, you can find a server that processes credit cards for a fixed rate.

Some servers have lower fees and rates but get a commission on the sale of your products in a type of partnership. Their profits rise with yours. They may charge as much as 10% of gross sales for posting your pages, taking orders over the Net, and forwarding them to your fulfillment facility. They get paid whether you get your money from the customer or not.

Some commercial servers charge a maintenance fee and percentage for credit card processing.

Some commercial servers have lower fees but take a commission on gross sales.

Checkups and Updates

You should check your posted documents over the Web periodically. Make sure the files are found at the URL you publicize, that they work correctly, and that the information is still up-to-date.

Things can go wrong over time as system administrators reconfigure servers. For example, files can be mistakenly deleted, renamed, or moved from the correct directory. If they are, links, graphics, and scripts will not work, especially if you used absolute path names.

Updates involve adding, deleting, or revising pages and links. You have to be certain that changes you make do not introduce any errors. Perform the tests you ran when first posting your pages (see page 164).

Update your files the same way you posted them to the server originally (see page 166). You can send them over the Internet if a few small files need updating. Be sure to arrange this with the system administrator.

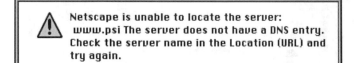

This message results from a bad server address in the URL.

Checkups add a few items to the normal testing procedure conducted before you posted the files.

- Is your home page located at the correct URL?

- Are the linked pages, graphics, and gateway scripts at the correct URLs?

- Do links work?

- Do graphics load?

- Do gateway scripts run?

- Do forms send input to the correct gateway script?

- Do responses, if any, return to browsers from gateway scripts?

- Do you get the correctly processed data from gateway scripts?

- Are links to other people's documents still valid URLs?

- Is the information still current and relevant?

- Are pointer pages in place for files that moved to new URLs?

- Do searchable indexes have your pages listed in their databases?

- What do usage reports from the server tell you about your document?

- Did you address issues brought to your attention by users? Your home page should have your e-mail address in case users find something wrong.

This message comes from a server that could not find the file you requested. The path or file name portion of the URL is incorrect.

How To Find Things on the Web

Automated search engines help you find things on the Web. *Search engines* are like the information booth at a mall; you tell the person at the booth what you are looking for, jewelry for example, and they give you a list of stores that may have what you need. They also show you where to find the stores in the mall.

All search engines work pretty much the same. You fill out a form that defines the search parameters and words you want to find, and the engine searches for URLs (file names), titles of documents, linked text, and URLs in linked text. When it completes the search, the results are displayed on your screen as links to the files that match your search criteria. You can then use the link to jump directly to the file.

Some search engines include many topics; others are limited to specific technical databases, individual journals, or libraries. Some searchable indexes are listed on the facing page. Some are slow but contain a wealth of information. Others are quick but less thorough. Find one that indexes the kind of information you are looking for. A search engine usually makes available an explanation of its content and method of compiling it.

Another way to find things on the Web is with the help of a directory. A *directory* is like the card catalog at a library or the table of contents in a book. You look through the lists of pages for one that interests you. Most of these are grouped into listings of related topics to help you find these by topics. The CERN W3 Servers, Yahoo, and EINet Galaxy pages listed on the next page include directories.

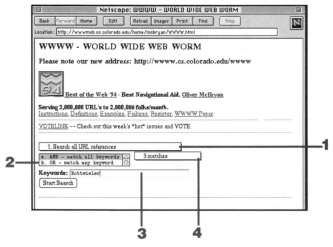

1 Choose part of the Web documents that you want the engine to search.

2 Choose one of the search methods.

3 Type the words you want to search for.

4 Choose the number of matches you want to see.

Some Web indexes

Search Engine	URI
AltaVista	**http://www.altavista.com**
Excite	**http://www.excite.com**
Infoseek	**http://www.infoseek.com**
Lycos	**http://lycos.com**
WebCrawler	**http://webcrawler.com**
Yahoo	**http://www.yahoo.com**

For a larger list of search engines and directories, see the W3 Search Engines page at **http://cuiwww.unige.ch/meta-index.html**.

The search engine returns the results as a list of links.

Getting Your Files Noticed

One way to get your files noticed by people browsing the Web is by listing them with searchable indexes (some of these indexes are listed on page 180). Find the ones that fit your audience: if your audience is wide, list files with a general interest index that includes many topics; if your readership is targeted, find an index limited to special interest areas.

You should check all indexes periodically for your files. Some indexes collect information automatically, others require you to submit your URLs to the database through a form. Conduct test searches that should result in matches to your files. Use words that other people would think of using, not the word you know results in a match. Remember, indexes search for URLs (file names), titles of documents (which are different from the file names), linked text, and URLs in linked text.

There are offline ways of getting noticed as well.

- Use traditional media for publicizing your files. People still read, listen to radio, and watch television news programs. Press releases can get you in those media.

- Advertise if you have the budget.

- Include the URL in the address block of any printed materials.

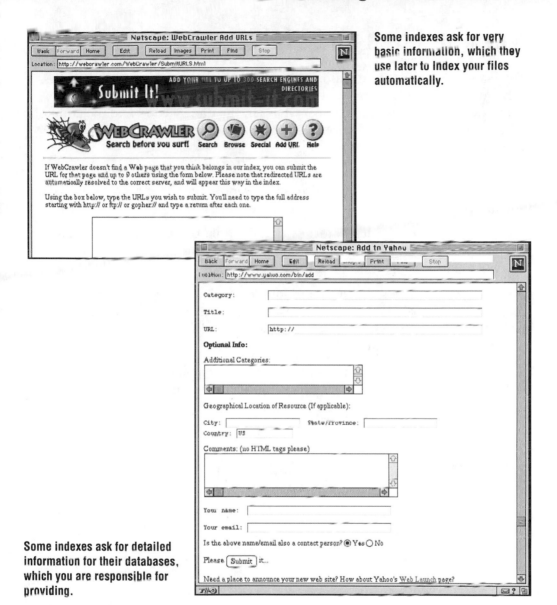

Some indexes ask for very basic information, which they use later to index your files automatically.

Some indexes ask for detailed information for their databases, which you are responsible for providing.

Naming Files and Links

There are at least two good reasons for using plain English when naming files, titles in headers, linked text, and URLs. First, you and those you work with won't need crib sheets to remember what's in the files. Second and most important, people find your files through searchable indexes that catalog the names you choose.

People think of words to search for the way they talk. They tend to try whole words first, like *Rottweiler, Abyssinian*, and *amortization* rather than *rtwlr, absinin,* and *amort*. Use common words whenever possible.

Indexes also catalog the actual text used as the link. Use linked text that has meaning. Linking the words *click this* for more on heart attacks won't do you much good in a search index. But linking the words *heart attack* will.

A naming system helps you keep track of files and makes updates easier. Clever naming systems based on abbreviations and numbers mean nothing to people unfamiliar with your system. They are meaningless in an index and are unlikely to ever come up in a search.

Some servers place constraints on the number of characters in a file name. Use short words and common abbreviations for file names on these servers.

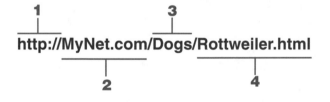

1 The http:// in front of an URL indicates a Web site.

2 A domain has a suffix that indicates what kind of organization runs the Web site.

3 Use slashes to separate any directory names.

4 Put the HTML file name at the end.

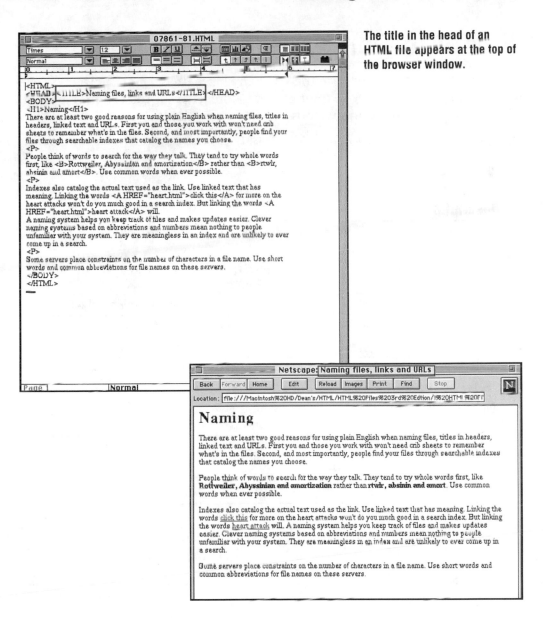

The title in the head of an HTML file appears at the top of the browser window.

07861-81.HTML

```
<HTML>
<HEAD><TITLE>Naming files, links and URLs</TITLE></HEAD>
<BODY>
<H1>Naming</H1>
There are at least two good reasons for using plain English when naming files, titles in
headers, linked text and URLs. First you and those you work with won't need crib
sheets to remember what's in the files. Second, and most importantly, people find your
files through searchable indexes that catalog the names you choose.
<P>
People think of words to search for the way they talk. They tend to try whole words
first, like <B>Rottweiler, Abyssinian and amortization</B> rather than <B>rtwlr,
absinin and amort</B>. Use common words when ever possible.
<P>
Indexes also catalog the actual text used as the link. Use linked text that has
meaning. Linking the words <A HREF="heart.html">click this</A> for more on the
heart attacks won't do you much good in a search index. But linking the words <A
HREF="heart.html">heart attack</A> will.
A naming system helps you keep track of files and makes updates easier. Clever
naming systems based on abbreviations and numbers mean nothing to people
unfamiliar with your system. They are meaningless in an index and are unlikely to ever
come up in a search.
<P>
Some servers place constraints on the number of characters in a file name. Use short
words and common abbreviations for file names on these servers.
</BODY>
</HTML>
```

Page 1   Normal

Netscape: Naming files, links and URLs

Back | Forward | Home | Edit | Reload | Images | Print | Find | Stop

Location: file:///Macintosh%20HD/Dean's/HTML/HTML%20Files%203rd%20Edtion/!%20HTML%20Fl

Naming

There are at least two good reasons for using plain English when naming files, titles in headers, linked text and URLs. First you and those you work with won't need crib sheets to remember what's in the files. Second, and most importantly, people find your files through searchable indexes that catalog the names you choose.

People think of words to search for the way they talk. They tend to try whole words first, like **Rottweiler, Abyssinian and amortization** rather than **rtwlr, absinin and amort**. Use common words when ever possible.

Indexes also catalog the actual text used as the link. Use linked text that has meaning. Linking the words click this for more on the heart attacks won't do you much good in a search index. But linking the words heart attack will. A naming system helps you keep track of files and makes updates easier. Clever naming systems based on abbreviations and numbers mean nothing to people unfamiliar with your system. They are meaningless in an index and are unlikely to ever come up in a search.

Some servers place constraints on the number of characters in a file name. Use short words and common abbreviations for file names on these servers.

Where To Find Software on the Web

Much of the software used with the Web is freeware (free) and shareware (you can download and try it for a limited time before paying). You can find most of this software at popular anonymous FTP sites or via the Web.

If you need Web browsers and HTML tools, here are some good places to look:

Windows Software

Description	URL
Mosaic and Viewers	ftp://ftp.ncsa.uiuc.edu/Web/Mosaic/Windows
HTML	ftp://ftp.ncsa.uiuc.edu/Web/html/Windows
Netscape	ftp://ftp.netscape.com/pub/navigator
W4 Server (Windows 3.1 and Win95)	http://130.89.224.16:69
Windows 3.1 httpd (Web Server)	http://www.city.net/win-httpd/
Windows 95 httpd (Web Server)	http://website.ora.com
Freeware HTTP Server for Windows NT	ftp://emwac.ed.ac.uk/pub/https/
Windows 95 software	http://www.windows95.com http://www.tucows.com

Macintosh Software

Description	URL
Mosaic and Viewers	ftp://ftp.ncsa.uiuc.edu/Web/Mosaic/Mac
HTML	ftp://ftp.ncsa.uiuc.edu/Web/html/Mac
HTML	ftp://ftp.hawaii.edu/mirrors/info-mac/TextProcessing/html
Netscape	ftp://ftp.netscape.com/pub/navigator
MacHTTP (Web Server)	http://www.biap.com/machttp/machttp_software.html

UNIX Software

Description	URL
Mosaic and Viewers	ftp://ftp.ncsa.uiuc.edu/Web/Mosaic/Unix

Description	URL
Netscape	ftp://ftp.netscape.com/pub/navigator
HTML	ftp://ftp.ncsa.uiuc.edu/Web/ html/hotmetal/SPARC-Motif
tkWWW (HTML and Web browser)	ftp://ftp.aud.alcatel.com/tcl/extensions/
NCSA httpd (Web Server)	http://hoohoo.ncsa.uiuc.edu/ docs/setup/Download.html
CERN HTTP (Web Server)	http://www.w3.org/hypertext/ WWW/Daemon/Status.html

If you need other types of software not directly related to the Web, check one of these other FTP sites with good collections:

Windows Software

Description	URL
Internet Software	ftp://ftp.cica.indiana.edu/pub/pc/
Microsoft	ftp://ftp.microsoft.com

Mac Software

Description	URL
Internet Software	ftp://ftp.hawaii.edu/mirrors/info- mac/Communication/MacTCP
More Internet Software	ftp://wuarchive.wustl.edu/systems/mac/ umich.edu

UNIX Software

Description	URL
UNIX Software	ftp://ftp.uu.net/systems/unix
UNIX Software	ftp://sunsite.unc.edu/pub/packages
UNIX Software	ftp://wuarchive.wustl.edu/systems/unix
Linux Software	ftp://wuarchive.wustl.edu/ systems.linux/sunsite

Glossary

Absolute path—Absolute paths spell out the location of a file by starting at the highest level and listing each directory needed to find the file itself.

AIFF—A common sound file format on the Macintosh.

Anchor—Text and graphics can link to places within the same document. These links require two parts: the anchor and the link. The anchor identifies the place to jump to.

Annotate—To provide descriptive text for a possibly vague item. For example, placing comments in an HTML document annotates the code by providing descriptions of what the code accomplishes.

Anonymous FTP—FTP transactions that do not require a unique login name or password. Use the name *anonymous* to log in and use your e-mail address as a password.

Applets—Small programs that accomplish a specific purpose. Applets usually act as supplemental programs for larger applications.

Argument—Words or numbers you enter as part of an HTML tag to expand or modify how that tag operates.

ASCII—Acronym for American Standard Code for Information Interchange, a standard character set.

Authoring software—Computer programs that aid in creating HTML documents by inserting the code for tags.

BODY—HTML tag used to enclose the body (all the text and tags) of the HTML document.

Browser—A program used to view HTML documents and navigate the World Wide Web. See *Netscape, Mosaic,* and *Lynx.*

Byte—Eight bits; the fundamental unit of personal computer data.

CERN—European Particle Physics Laboratory, the developers of the World Wide Web.

CGI—(Common Gateway Interface) The scripting language used to write gateway scripts for CERN and NCSA Web servers.

Check boxes—Used in forms to make it possible to select one or more non-exclusive options in a list.

Coordinates—Pairs of numbers used to define the edges of the clickable areas in image maps.

Dedicated connection—Access to the Internet that is always available via a special connection such as FDDI, T1, or switched 56. See *dial-up connections* and *ISDN.*

Default—The initial value of any input type (text field, check box, radio button, selection list) used in a form.

Dial-up connections—Accessing the Internet by means of a modem and communication software.

Directory—A major division on a hard drive or server used to divide and organize files.

Domain—The name for a company, organization, or individual's Internet connection. Individual computers within this domain all end with the domain as part of their host name.

Download—To transfer a file from another computer to your computer.

E-mail (electronic mail)—A communication system that allows you to send an electronic "letter" to one or more recipients.

Ethernet—A standard for local area network hardware, cabling, and transmission.

External files—Any files that are not directly loadable by a browser such as some image formats, sounds, videos, or even program files.

FDDI—A type of high-speed dedicated connection to the Internet with a speed of 45 M/sec.

File formats—The patterns and standards used to store a program on a disk. Examples are GIF, JPEG, AIFF.

Font—The name of a particular typeface. For example, Times Roman Bold is a font.

Form—HTML documents designed with fill-in text boxes, lists of options, and other elements that allow the user of the form to send information back to the Web server.

Freeware—Software that is distributed at no cost to the user. (The author maintains the copyright.)

FTP (File Transfer Protocol)—The primary method for accessing files via the Internet.

Gateway script—A program that is run on a Web server that processes the input from forms.

GIF—A popular type of image file format.

Gopher—A menu-based information system on the Internet popularized because of its ability to interconnect different Gopher sites on the same menu.

Graphical browser—A program used to view formatted HTML documents and navigate the World Wide Web. Graphical browsers can display inline images and display text in various type styles. Examples are Mosaic and Netscape.

Gutter—The space between textual columns. Occasionally, gutter is also used to define the space between a column and the edge of a page.

Head—The HTML tag used to enclose the beginning elements in the HTML document, including the title.

Home page—The first HTML document that you intend people to see at your Web site is known as a home page.

Host name—The name of a computer on the Internet, used to identify it in the URL naming scheme.

HTML (Hypertext Markup Language)—The coding scheme used to format text for use on the World Wide Web.

HTTP (Hypertext Transport Protocol)—The transmission standard used to send HTML documents across the World Wide Web.

Hypertext—An interlinked document structure that allows you to jump freely from one topic or document to another.

Internet—The general term used to describe the worldwide network of computers and services encompassing some 20–40 million computer users and dozens of information systems including e-mail, Gopher, FTP, and the World Wide Web.

Internet access fees—Costs charged by Internet access providers to connect to the Internet.

Internet access provider—A company that sells connections to the Internet to other companies and individuals. Also called *Internet service provider*.

ISDN (Integrated Services Digital Network)—A high-speed dial-up connection to the Internet. Availability and cost are determined in part by local telephone companies.

Java—A C-like programming language developed by Sun Microsystems to allow object oriented programming on Web pages.

Linear document—A type of organization for HTML documents in which one HTML file follows the next. The HTML author determines the order in which the information is presented.

Link—The text or graphic used in an HTML document to jump from one document to another.

LiveAudio—A Plug-In developed by Netscape to play various sound files in their browser. LiveAudio ships with Netscape and is installed when you install the browser.

Load time—The amount of time it takes a user to retrieve a Web page and view it in a browser.

LocalTalk—A local area network standard used by Macintosh computers.

Lynx—A non-graphical browser for UNIX and DOS systems. See also *Netscape* and *Mosaic*.

Macintosh—A brand of personal computers manufactured by Apple Computer.

Menu—An on-screen display that lists available choices.

Method—The manner in which an HTML form is submitted to the Web server. The most common method is *post*.

MIDI—Musical Instrument Digital Interface. A standard that allows digital instruments to talk to and control one another. On a computer, MIDI files can contain musical scores that can be reproduced on a sound card.

Modem—A device that converts digital information from a computer to analog information that can be sent over telephone lines. This allows computers equipped with modems to communicate over telephone lines.

Monospaced font—A typeface in which the width of each character is the same.

Mosaic—One of the first graphical browsers. Developed by the NCSA, this browser fueled the growth of the Web. It is available in versions for Windows, Mac, and UNIX.

MPEG (Motion Picture Experts Group)—A standard and file format for motion video on computers.

Multimedia—Documents that combine text, graphics, sound, movies, or other media.

Named entity—Special characters whose HTML code is an ampersand (&) followed by a name.

NCSA (National Center for Supercomputing Applications)—The research group that developed Mosaic, a popular graphical browser.

Netscape—A popular commercial graphical browser. It is available in versions for Windows, Mac, and UNIX.

Network administrator—The person responsible for maintaining a network and assisting its users.

Non-graphical browser—A program used to view HTML documents and navigate the World Wide Web. Non-graphical browsers do not display inline images and do not display formatted text. An example is *Lynx*.

Non-linear document—A type of organization for HTML documents in which one HTML file contains links to more than one other HTML file. The person browsing the files determines the order in which the information is presented.

Numbered entity—Special characters whose HTML code is an ampersand (&) followed by a number.

Operating system—A master control program for a computer. Examples are DOS, UNIX, and the MacOS. (Technically speaking, Microsoft Windows 3.x is an operating environment as it still requires the separate DOS operating system to run. Microsoft's Windows 95 is a true operating system as DOS is built into it.)

Paired Tags—Two tags that must be used in conjunction with each other, usually to surround elements on which they operate. For example, **<FONT>** and **</FONT>** are paired font tags. Also referred to as container tags.

Parameters—A set of values passed to an external program to control its operation.

Path name—The place where a file is stored on a computer, indicated by the drive or volume name and the subdirectories needed to find the file. See *relative path* and *absolute path*.

Photoshop—A high-end graphics editing program by Adobe, more common on Macintosh computers.

Pixels—The smallest measure of the image on a computer screen. Each individual dot of light is a pixel.

Platform—A computer hardware standard, such as IBM PC compatible or Macintosh.

Plug-ins—Small programs that can be installed to extend a browser's capabilities. Plug-ins are usually developed by third parties so HTML browsers can display their proprietary data files. For example, the ShockWave Plug-in was developed by Macromedia so that Netscape could display Macromedia Director animation files.

Polygon—A closed shape of three or more sides—triangles, rectangles, octagons, and so on.

Post—To place an HTML file on a Web server to make it available for browsing.

Preference setting—Program options in browsers that allow the user to determine such things as which fonts are used for various HTML styles, whether or not inline images are displayed, what other applications are used to view movies, and so on.

Proportional font—A typeface in which the width of each character varies depending on the character's shape. An *I* takes up less space than a *w* for example.

Public domain software—Software that is made freely available by the developer and which the developer gives up all copyright ownership to.

QuarkXPress—A high-end page layout program used on the Macintosh.

Quicktime—A standard video image format, popular on the Macintosh, but also available on the PC.

Radio button—Used in forms to make it possible to select one exclusive option in a list.

RAM (random access memory)—The computer's primary working memory in which program instructions and data are stored.

Relative path—Relative paths spell out the location of a file based on the current document location.

Rollover—A term used to define when the mouse pointer is moved to point at a given object on the screen. Generally, this refers to an event that happens when the mouse pointer is placed on a specific object.

Router—A device connecting a LAN to the Internet that routes transmissions between the two.

Sans Serif—A type of font that lacks decorative scrollwork on its letters. This font is Serif (has decorative scrollwork), while this font is Sans Serif (no scrollwork).

Scripts—A set of instructions that tell someone or something what to do. In HTML, scripts are small programs that can be placed on a Web page to add interactivity and to help control the page. JavaScript is one such "scripting" language.

Scroll—To move a large image around on the screen in order to view it.

Searchable index—Indexes of World Wide Web documents that you can submit a query to and the index searches to find pages matching your specification.

Serif—A type of font that has decorative scrollwork on its letters. This font is Serif (has decorative scrollwork), while this font is Sans Serif (no scrollwork).

Server—See *Web server*.

Shareware—Software that you can obtain for free (often by downloading from the Internet) on a trial basis but that may require some payment or registration for continued used.

Sound board—Hardware used to play sound files on computers.

Submit—To send a completed form to a Web server.

T1—A high-speed dedicated connection to the Internet that provides data transmission rates of 1.5 M/sec.

Tag—The HTML codes used to specify text styles, links, graphics, and other HTML elements.

Target—The area on the screen where specific text is directed. This term is used mostly with frames when a specific document is meant to be displayed in a specific frame.

Text fields—Form elements that allow users to insert a single line of text.

TITLE—The HTML tag used to give each HTML document a title.

Transmission line—The physical connection from your computer to the Internet such as a telephone line or a T1.

Transparent graphics—Graphic images that have a clear background, which makes the graphic appear to float in the browser screen.

Typeface—The distinctive design of the letter of a specific type style. The typeface is also uniquely determined by its size, style, weight, and posture.

UNIX—An operating system used on a variety of computers from personal computers to mainframe. Many computers and servers connected to the Internet use UNIX.

URL (Uniform Resource Locator)— The standard used to identify files on the Internet and World Wide Web using the type of server, the host name of the computer the file is on, and the complete path to the file.

Video board—Hardware used to play movie files on computers.

Visual Basic—A programming language by Microsoft modeled after the BASIC programming language. Visual Basic is popular because of its easy-to-use, graphical, drag-and-drop programming interface. (Hence the name *Visual*.)

WAV—A popular sound file format used primarily by Windows-based computers.

Web server—The hardware and software used to store and deliver HTML documents for use on the World Wide Web.

Web site—A person or company's collection of HTML documents on a Web server. A single Web server may contain one or more Web sites.

Windows—An operating environment for the IBM PC-compatible platform that allows several programs to run at once and utilizes icons and menus for program control.

Word processor—A program used to create and edit text documents. When using a word processor to create HTML documents, save the documents as ASCII text rather than in the word processor's proprietary format.

World Wide Web (WWW)—An Internet service that links multimedia documents together using hypertext. Users can jump between documents using links to view text, graphics, movies, and other media.

ASCII Codes

Decimal	Name	Character	Decimal	Name	Character
0	blank		31	down triangle	▼
1	happy face	☺	32	space	Space
2	inverse happy face	●	33	exclamation point	!
3	heart	♥	34	quotation mark	"
4	diamond	♦	35	number sign	#
5	club	♣	36	dollar sign	$
6	spade	♠	37	percent sign	%
7	bullet	•	38	ampersand	&
8	inverse bullet	◘	39	apostrophe	'
9	circle	o	40	opening parenthesis	(
10	inverse circle	◙	41	closing parenthesis	)
11	male sign	♂	42	asterisk	*
12	female sign	♀	43	plus sign	+
13	single note	♪	44	comma	,
14	double note	♫	45	hyphen or minus sign	-
15	sun	☼	46	period	.
16	right triangle	►	47	slash	/
17	left triangle	◄	48	zero	0
18	up/down arrow	↕	49	one	1
19	double exclamation	!!	50	two	2
20	paragraph sign	¶	51	three	3
21	section sign	§	52	four	4
22	rectangular bullet	■	53	five	5
23	up/down to line	↨	54	six	6
24	up arrow	↑	55	seven	7
25	down arrow	↓	56	eight	8
26	right arrow	→	57	nine	9
27	left arrow	←	58	colon	:
28	lower left box	∟	59	semicolon	;
29	left/right arrow	↔	60	less-than sign	<
30	up triangle	▲			

Decimal	Name	Character	Decimal	Name	Character
61	equal sign	=	97	lowercase A	a
62	greater-than sign	>	98	lowercase B	b
63	question mark	?	99	lowercase C	c
64	at sign	@	100	lowercase D	d
65	capital A	A	101	lowercase E	e
66	capital B	B	102	lowercase F	f
67	capital C	C	103	lowercase G	g
68	capital D	D	104	lowercase H	h
69	capital E	E	105	lowercase I	i
70	capital F	F	106	lowercase J	j
71	capital G	G	107	lowercase K	k
72	capital H	H	108	lowercase L	l
73	capital I	I	109	lowercase M	m
74	capital J	J	110	lowercase N	n
75	capital K	K	111	lowercase O	o
76	capital L	L	112	lowercase P	p
77	capital M	M	113	lowercase Q	q
78	capital N	N	114	lowercase R	r
79	capital O	O	115	lowercase S	s
80	capital P	P	116	lowercase T	t
81	capital Q	Q	117	lowercase U	u
82	capital R	R	118	lowercase V	v
83	capital S	S	119	lowercase W	w
84	capital T	T	120	lowercase X	x
85	capital U	U	121	lowercase Y	y
86	capital V	V	122	lowercase Z	z
87	capital W	W	123	opening brace	{
88	capital X	X	124	vertical line	|
89	capital Y	Y	125	closing brace	}
90	capital Z	Z	126	tilde	~
91	opening bracket	[	127	small house	⌂
92	backward slash	\	128	C cedilla	Ç
93	closing bracket	]	129	u umlaut	ü
94	caret	^	130	e acute	é
95	underscore	_	131	a circumflex	â
96	grave	`			

(continues)

Decimal	Name	Character
132	a umlaut	ä
133	a grave	à
134	a ring	å
135	c cedilla	ç
136	e circumflex	ê
137	e umlaut	ë
138	e grave	è
139	I umlaut	Ï
140	I circumflex	Î
141	I grave	Ì
142	A umlaut	Ä
143	A ring	Å
144	E acute	É
145	ae ligature	æ
146	AE ligature	Æ
147	o circumflex	ô
148	o umlaut	ö
149	o grave	ò
150	u circumflex	û
151	u grave	ù
152	y umlaut	ÿ
153	O umlaut	Ö
154	U umlaut	Ü
155	cent sign	¢
156	pound sign	£
157	yen sign	¥
158	Pt	₧
159	function	ƒ
160	a acute	á
161	I acute	í
162	o acute	ó
163	u acute	ú
164	n tilde	ñ
165	N tilde	Ñ
166	a macron	ª
167	o macron	º

Decimal	Name	Character
168	opening question mark	¿
169	upper left box	⌐
170	upper right box	¬
171	1/2	½
172	1/4	¼
173	opening exclamation	¡
174	opening guillemets	«
175	closing guillemets	»
176	light block	░
177	medium block	▒
178	dark block	▓
179	single vertical	│
180	single right junction	┤
181	2 to 1 right junction	╡
182	1 to 2 right junction	╢
183	1 to 2 upper right	╖
184	2 to 1 upper right	╕
185	double right junction	╣
186	double vertical	║
187	double upper right	╗
188	double lower right	╝
189	1 to 2 lower right	╜
190	2 to 1 lower right	╛
191	single upper right	┐
192	single lower left	└
193	single lower junction	┴
194	single upper junction	┬
195	single left junction	├
196	single horizontal	─
197	single intersection	┼

Decimal	Name	Character	Decimal	Name	Character
198	2 to 1 left junction	⊢	229	sigma	σ
199	1 to 2 left junction	⊩	230	mu	μ
200	double lower left	⊑	231	tau	τ
201	double upper left	⊓	232	Phi	Φ
202	double lower junction	⟂	233	theta	θ
203	double upper junction	⟙	234	Omega	Ω
204	double left junction	⊪	235	delta	δ
205	double horizontal	=	236	infinity	∞
206	double intersection	⊬	237	phi	σ
207	1 to 2 lower junction	⟂	238	epsilon	ε
208	2 to 1 lower junction	⊥	239	intersection of sets	∩
209	1 to 2 upper junction	⊤	240	is identical to	≡
210	2 to 1 upper junction	π	241	plus/minus sign	±
211	1 to 2 lower left	├	242	greater/equal sign	≥
212	2 to 1 lower left	╘	243	less/equal sign	≤
213	2 to 1 upper left	╞	244	top half integral	⌠
214	1 to 2 upper left	π	245	lower half integral	⌡
215	2 to 1 intersection	╫	246	divide-by sign	÷
216	1 to 2 intersection	╪	247	approximately	≈
217	single lower right	┘	248	degree	°
218	single upper right	┌	249	filled-in degree	·
219	inverse space	■	250	small bullet	·
220	lower inverse	▬	251	square root	√
221	left inverse	▌	252	superscript n	n
222	right inverse	▌	253	superscript 2	2
223	upper inverse	▬	254	box	■
224	alpha	α	255	phantom space	
225	beta	β			
226	Gamma	Γ			
227	pi	π			
228	Sigma	Σ			

HTML Code by Type

Tag Name	Code	Page
Document Structure		
Body	<BODY>	20
Frame Definition	<FRAME>	68
Frame Setup	<FRAMESET>	69
Head	<HEAD>	20
HTML	<HTML>	20
Multiple Columns	<MULTICOL>	41a
No Frame Alternative	<NOFRAME>	68
Titles and Headings		
Heading - First Level	<H1>	20
Heading - Second Level	<H2>	20
Heading - Third Level	<H3>	20
Heading - Fourth Level	<H4>	20
Heading - Fifth Level	<H5>	20
Heading - Sixth Level	<H6>	20
Title	<Title>	20
Paragraphs and Lines		
Break	
	30
Horizontal Rule	<HR>	54
Paragraph	<P>	30
Styles	<STYLE>	17
Table	<TABLE>	58
Links		
Anchor	<A NAME="*name*">	48
Link	<A>	34
Link to an anchor	<A NAME="*anchor name*">	48
Link to another document	<A HREF="*filename*">	48
Linked graphic	<A HREF="*link filename*">	38
	<IMG SRC="*graphic filename*">	38
Linked text	<A HREF="*link filename*">*text to click*</A>	34

Tag Name	Code	Page
Character Formats		
Address	<ADDRESS>	22
Blockquote	<BLOCKQUOTE>	52
Bold	<B>	28
Code Sample	<CODE>	22
Emphasis	<EM>	22
Font Type/Color/Size	<FONT>	15
Italic	<I>	28
Keyboard	<KBD>	22
Preformatted Type	<PRE>	72
Strong	<STRONG>	22
Subscript	<SUB>	12
Superscript	<SUP>	12
Typewriter	<TT>	28
Underscore	<U>	28
Graphics		
Alternate to Image	<ALT>	46
"Browser Image Map Shapes"	<AREA SHAPE="[rect,circle,polygon]" COORDS="list of coordinates" HREF="filename">	45
Image Alignment	<IMG ALIGN=*[top, middle, bottom]* SRC="*filename*">	58
Image map	<IMG SRC="*image filename*" ISMAP>	76
Images	<IMG SRC="*filename*"	56
Spacer	<SPACER>	20
Video Images	<IMG DYNSRC="filename">	43
Lists		
Definition Lists	See *Glossary Lists*	68
Glossary List Definitions	<DD>	68
Glossary Lists	<DL>	68
Glossary List Terms	<DT>	68
List Item	<LI>	66
Ordered List	<OL>	66
Unordered List	<UL>	66

Tag Name	Code	Page
Forms		
Check box	\<input type="checkbox" name="*name*" value="*value*" [checked]\>	92
Form	\<FORM\>	84
Image Buttons	\<INPUT TYPE="IMAGE" SRC="filename" NAME="name" VALUE="value"\>	57
Pop-up list name	\<select name="*name*"\>	94
Pop-up list option	\<option\>	94
Pop-up list selected option	\<option selected\>	94
Radio button	\<input type="radio" name="*name*" value="*value*"[checked]\>	90
Reset button	\<input type=reset value="Clear"\>	84
Selection List	See *Pop-up List name*	94
Submit button	\<input type=submit value="Submit"\>	84
Text Field	\<input type="text" size="*xx*" name="*name*" maxlength="*yy*" value="*default*"\>	86
Objects, Scripts, and Applications		
Embedded Object	\<EMBED\>	48
No Embed Alternative	\<NOEMBED\>	48
Script/Applet	\<APPLET CODE="filename" WIDTH="width" HEIGHT="height"\>	47
Script/Applet Parameters	\<PARAM\>	47
Script Language	\<SCRIPT LANGUAGE="language"\>	46
Other Tags		
Background Sound	\<BGSOUND\>	37
Comment	\<!-*comment*-\>	122
Marquee	\<MARQUEE\>	18
Special Characters	&*character code*;	70

Color Names

Netscape and Internet Explorer both support the sixteen named colors shown in the table below. You can use the names of the colors instead of their RGB values in hexadecimal notation (for example, "#c0c0c0") in any tag that supports a color value. For example, the two tags:

<BODY BGCOLOR="#800080">

 and

< BODY BGCOLOR="Purple">

are identical.

Ease of identification in your HTML code is the main advantage of using color names instead of their corresponding values. For example, it is much easier to tell which color is specified when you see "Teal" as opposed to "#008080."

You may still want to use hexadecimal notation to define colors if the named color is not quite right. Each red, green, and blue component color has 256 values from 0, the darkest, to 255, the lightest. These must be expressed as hexadecimal doublets. Hexadecimal means base 16. Instead of counting 0 1 2 3 4 5 6 7 8 9 10 11 12 13 14 15, as we do in base ten, you count 0 1 2 3 4 5 6 7 8 9 a b c d e f. That means f in hexadecimal notation = 15 in base ten. 11 in hexadecimal notation = 17 in base ten, that is to say, one 16 + one 1 = 17.

Color Name	RGB Value
Black	#000000
Navy	#000080
Silver	#C0C0C0
Blue	#0000FF
Maroon	#800000
Purple	#800080
Red	#FF0000
Fuchsia	#FF00FF
Green	#008000
Teal	#008080
Lime	#00FF00
Aqua	#00FFFF

Color Name	RGB Value
Olive	#808000
Gray	#808080
Yellow	#FFFF00
White	#FFFFFF

Index

Index

Complete and Return this Card
for a *FREE* Computer Book Catalog

Thank you for purchasing this book! You have purchased a superior computer book written expressly for your needs. To continue to provide the kind of up-to-date, pertinent coverage you've come to expect from us, we need to hear from you. Please take a minute to complete and return this self-addressed, postage-paid form. In return, we'll send you a free catalog of all our computer books on topics ranging from word processing to programming and the internet.

Mr. ☐   Mrs. ☐   Ms. ☐   Dr. ☐

Name (first) ☐☐☐☐☐☐☐☐☐☐☐ (M.I.) ☐ (last) ☐☐☐☐☐☐☐☐☐☐☐☐☐☐☐☐☐

Address ☐☐☐☐☐☐☐☐☐☐☐☐☐☐☐☐☐☐☐☐☐☐☐☐☐☐☐☐

☐☐☐☐☐☐☐☐☐☐☐☐☐☐☐☐☐☐☐☐☐☐☐☐☐☐☐☐

City ☐☐☐☐☐☐☐☐☐☐☐   State ☐☐   Zip ☐☐☐☐☐ ☐☐☐☐

Phone ☐☐☐ ☐☐☐ ☐☐☐☐   Fax ☐☐☐ ☐☐☐ ☐☐☐☐

Company Name ☐☐☐☐☐☐☐☐☐☐☐☐☐☐☐☐☐☐☐☐☐☐☐☐☐

E-mail address ☐☐☐☐☐☐☐☐☐☐☐☐☐☐☐☐☐☐☐☐☐☐☐☐☐

1. Please check at least (3) influencing factors for purchasing this book.

Front or back cover information on book .... ☐
Special approach to the content .... ☐
Completeness of content .... ☐
Author's reputation .... ☐
Publisher's reputation .... ☐
Book cover design or layout .... ☐
Index or table of contents of book .... ☐
Price of book .... ☐
Special effects, graphics, illustrations .... ☐
Other (Please specify): _____ ☐

2. How did you first learn about this book?

Saw in Macmillan Computer Publishing catalog .... ☐
Recommended by store personnel .... ☐
Saw the book on bookshelf at store .... ☐
Recommended by a friend .... ☐
Received advertisement in the mail .... ☐
Saw an advertisement in: _____ ☐
Read book review in: _____ ☐
Other (Please specify): _____ ☐

3. How many computer books have you purchased in the last six months?

This book only .... ☐   3 to 5 books .... ☐
2 books .... ☐   More than 5 .... ☐

4. Where did you purchase this book?

Bookstore .... ☐
Computer Store .... ☐
Consumer Electronics Store .... ☐
Department Store .... ☐
Office Club .... ☐
Warehouse Club .... ☐
Mail Order .... ☐
Direct from Publisher .... ☐
Internet site .... ☐
Other (Please specify): _____ ☐

5. How long have you been using a computer?

☐ Less than 6 months   ☐ 6 months to a year
☐ 1 to 3 years   ☐ More than 3 years

6. What is your level of experience with personal computers and with the subject of this book?

	With PCs	With subject of book
New	☐	☐
Casual	☐	☐
Accomplished	☐	☐
Expert	☐	☐

Source Code ISBN: 0-0000-0000-0

**7. Which of the following best describes your
   job title?**

Administrative Assistant .... ☐
Coordinator .... ☐
Manager/Supervisor .... ☐
Director .... ☐
Vice President .... ☐
President/CEO/COO .... ☐
Lawyer/Doctor/Medical Professional .... ☐
Teacher/Educator/Trainer .... ☐
Engineer/Technician .... ☐
Consultant .... ☐
Not employed/Student/Retired .... ☐
Other (Please specify): _____ ☐

**8. Which of the following best describes the area of
   the company your job title falls under?**

Accounting .... ☐
Engineering .... ☐
Manufacturing .... ☐
Operations .... ☐
Marketing .... ☐
Sales .... ☐
Other (Please specify): _____ ☐

9. What is your age?

Under 20 .... ☐
21-29 .... ☐
30-39 .... ☐
40-49 .... ☐
50-59 .... ☐
60-over .... ☐

10. Are you:

Male .... ☐
Female .... ☐

**11. Which computer publications do you read
   regularly? (Please list)**

_____
_____
_____
_____
_____
_____
_____
_____
_____

Comments: _____
_____
_____

Fold here and scotch-tape to mail.

MACMILLAN COMPUTER PUBLISHING USA

A VIACOM COMPANY

Technical Support:

If you need assistance with the information in this book or with a CD/Disk accompanying the book, please access the Knowledge Base on our Web site at **http://www.superlibrary.com/general/support**. Our most Frequently Asked Questions are answered there. If you do not find the answer to your questions on our Web site, you may contact Macmillan Technical Support **(317) 581-3833** or e-mail us at **support@mcp.com**.

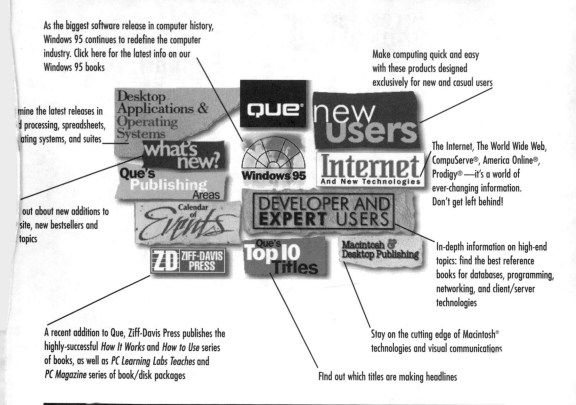